HOUSING WEALTH

FIRST TIMERS TO OLD TIMERS

DOMINIC MAXWELL AND SONIA SODHA

ippr

The **Institute for Public Policy Research** (ippr) is the UK's leading progressive think tank and was established in 1988. Its role is to bridge the political divide between the social democratic and liberal traditions, the intellectual divide between academia and the policy making establishment and the cultural divide between government and civil society. It is first and foremost a research institute, aiming to provide innovative and credible policy solutions. Its work, the questions its research poses and the methods it uses are driven by the belief that the journey to a good society is one that places social justice, democratic participation and economic and environmental sustainability at its core.

For further information you can contact ippr's external affairs department on info@ippr.org, you can view our website at www.ippr.org and you can buy our books from Central Books on 0845 458 9910 or email ippr@centralbooks.com.

Our trustees

© IPPR 2006

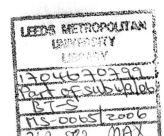

CONTENTS

Acknowledgements

This project would not have been possible without generous support from Prudential, Places for People, Standard Life Bank and the Yorkshire Building Society. We are also grateful to The Children's Mutual and HBOS for their support of ippr's Centre for Asset-Based Welfare.

Helpful comments on this and previous versions were received from Sue Adams, Jim Bennett, Anthony Burn, Christine Heffernan, Ian Kearns, Adam Marshall, Simon Maxwell, Jennifer Rankin, Nick Pearce, Peter Robinson, Howard Reed, Sue Regan, Kate Stanley, Anthony Vigor and Steve Wilcox. Will Paxton helped to set up the project.

Helpful discussions were also held with Andy Caton, Carl Bennet, Glen Bramley, Alan Burnett, Chris Curry, Peter Fisher, Alban Hawksworth, Keith Haggart, John Hills, Mervyn Kohler, Donald Hirsch, Ged Hosty, Ian McNeil, Ken MacIntyre, Joanne Seagars, Lisa Sutcliffe and John Slaughter.

Invaluable research support was provided by Lula Durant, Kayte Lawton, Emma Street and Irina Polonsky.

To all of the above, to the attendees at our seminars, and to the many others who helped us in our research – thank you. Any remaining errors are the responsibility of the authors.

About this project

As part of this project, we held four seminars with policy experts and prac-titioners, including one with the Joseph Rowntree Foundation, and one roundtable discussion with the then Parliamentary Under-Secretary of State for Social Exclusion, Yvette Cooper. Practitioners and product providers were consulted at other stages in the project. We also conducted focus groups and in-depth interviews with asset-rich, income-poor pensioners of different ages to investigate the attitudes of this group towards different methods of releasing wealth from the home.

Two working papers were published as part of the project. *Shifting Foundations: Home Ownership and Government Objectives* by Dominic Maxwell considered the case for government support of policies to increase access to homeownership. *Housing-Rich, Income-Poor: the potential of housing wealth in old age* by Sonia Sodha analysed data from the 2002-03 English Longitudinal Study of Ageing on the number of asset-rich, income-poor pensioners. Both are available at www.ippr.org.

About the authors

Dominic Maxwell is a research fellow in the social policy team at ippr, hav-ing joined in 2004. His previous publications have covered asset-based wel-fare, including Child Trust Funds and financial inclusion; wealth inequal-ity; reform of inheritance tax; land value taxation; and the politics of the flat tax. Before joining ippr he was a research assistant for a Labour MP, and has previous experience at HM Treasury and Progress. He has a BA (Hons) in Philosophy, Politics and Economics from the University of Oxford.

Sonia Sodha is a research assistant in the social policy team at ippr. Before joining ippr, she worked for the Social Market Foundation and the Race Equality Unit at the Home Office. She has an MPhil in Politics and a BA (Hons) in Philosophy, Politics and Economics from the University of Oxford. She has published previously on Child Trust Funds and housing wealth.

Executive summary

Housing wealth is important, and it will become more so. Historically, it has been an excellent investment for those who have been able to own, and, by 2003, accounted for just over 50 per cent of net personal wealth (HM Revenue and Customs 2006b).

But the role that housing wealth can play has been overstated. To improve access to housing wealth, the priority for government should be building an assets ladder, rather than a housing ladder:

- If the motivation is *fairness and equality*, the first task should be to help those at the very bottom.
- If the motivation is helping people to *acquire wealth*, homeownership is less profitable and more risky for those on lower incomes.
- If the motivation is helping people to benefit from the *psycho-social effects of owning wealth*, financial assets appear to offer clearer gains than housing wealth, for both individuals and communities.

Therefore the Government should ensure that people on low incomes have decent incentives to save, rather than looking at homeownership in isolation.

In the past, homeownership has been profitable largely because of windfall increases in land value, redistributing wealth from non-owners to owners. Preventing this requires a renewed commitment to regional policy, using the charged issue of homeownership to increase its public priority. And it requires a clear argument from government that recent house price gains have created losers as well as winners, and the taxation of windfall housing wealth is a fair way of paying for the measures needed to address the gap.

Later in life, many look to their home to provide income in retirement. In fact, one fifth of retired people living in poverty own more than £100,000 of housing wealth. This amounts to 440,000 retired people, 4.4 per cent of the overall retired population, each owning an average of £177,000 of housing wealth, or £77.1 billion in total.

The potential of housing wealth to meet other needs is relatively restricted. A house provides rent-free living in retirement, but, for the vast majority of homeowners, a house should not be thought of as a pension. That said, for those who do want to release wealth from their home in retirement, there are important barriers that government can help to overcome.

- *Means testing* in the benefits system unfairly penalises the transfer of wealth from housing to liquid savings, and should be reduced. Almost a million pensioners, 8.2 per cent, own more than £100,000 of equiv-alised housing wealth, but are on means-tested benefits. Previous research from ippr has shown that a fairer system is possible (Brooks *et al* 2002).

- *Financial advice* available to older people wanting to buy equity release products is expensive and often of low quality. As such, there is a strong argument for government provision of generic financial advice for older people in order to fill this gap.
- *A lack of suitable properties to move into* hampers older people's ability to trade down. Half of low-income retired homeowners live in 'larger homes', meaning at least three rooms, in addition to a kitchen, bath-room(s), one bedroom for the first one or two household members and one further bedroom for each additional member.
- *Logistical problems* associated with moving house, particularly for the 'old old', can trap asset-rich, income-poor pensioners in unsuitable homes.

Aside from these four sets of actions, there is not a strong case for govern-ment actively supporting the market for equity release.

Summary of key recommendations

To help younger households, the Government should:
- ensure that those on low incomes have decent *incentives to save*, perhaps through a national rollout of the Saving Gateway pilots.
- use the charged issue of homeownership to increase the priority the pub-lic gives to *associated issues*, especially regional policy, the transmission of wealth inequality across generations, and the taxation of windfall hous-ing wealth, which should be defended as a fair way of paying for the measures needed to help those who are made worse off by house price inflation.
- exercise caution in how *mixed communities* are achieved in existing social housing developments. Artificially shifting tenants into homeownership cannot be expected to deliver the benefits of mixed communities: mixed tenure is a condition, not a cause, of mixed communities.

The case for government support of equity release is weak, and releasing housing wealth will remain expensive. But there are actions that the gov-ernment should take.

To reduce benefit disincentives, the Government should:
- tackle the arbitrary penalties to releasing wealth from the home for pen-sioners on benefits, as part of pensions reform following the Pensions

White Paper in May 2006. Previous research by ippr has shown that it is possible and desirable to eliminate Pension Credit and replace it with a non-means-tested British State Pension at the level of guarantee credit (£114.05 per week for a single pensioner in 2006-07) (Brooks *et al* 2002, Paxton *et al* 2005).

To improve advice, the Government should:
- establish a *generic financial advice service*, 'MoneyDoctor', to cater specifically for older people. This should provide a combination of telephone and face-to-face advice, and carry strong independent branding. It could be augmented by providing the infrastructure for *pro bono* work by independent financial advisers, and by encouraging contributions from firms who would benefit from reducing public distrust of equity release. It could also include financial health checks at retirement that include looking at housing options, and making clear, where appropriate, the benefits of moving early.
- make available a free, online *benefits calculator* for pensioners so they can calculate the effects of increasing their income or capital on their benefit eligibility. This should be simple and transparent, so it can be used by individuals as well as financial intermediaries.
- undertake an annual *mystery shopping exercise* of financial advisers offering advice on equity release, through the FSA. This would act as a deterrent to advisers who may be cutting corners, and provide regular snapshots on the quality of advice.

To increase the supply of housing suitable for older people, the Government should:
- give a stronger focus to older people in the new version of the *Planning Policy Statement 3*, and an explicit focus in the revised *Section 106* agreements between local authorities and developers.

To help older retired people trade down, the Government should:
- provide *logistical help trading down*, building on the lessons learnt in the 'Should I Stay or Should I Go?' pilots and elsewhere. This means that the Supporting People budget must be fairly allocated to services that meet the needs of retired low-income homeowners. The 2005 Pre-Budget Report cut the budget for the fourth year in a row.
- widen *adaptation grants*, by extending the remit of home improvement agencies to include housing options and move-on services.

Housing is an asset like no other. It has fed wealth inequality, transmitting disadvantage from one generation to the next. At the same time, those who do want to use housing wealth in older age face high costs to doing so. This book argues that the answer does not lie in subsidies at either end of the lifecycle, either to support first-time buyers or to subsidise the release of equity. Instead, the Government should be prioritising an assets ladder over a housing ladder, to ensure that the asset buffer that is necessary for sustainable homeownership is more easily obtainable for those on low incomes; and it should facilitate the release of wealth by reducing the tangled complexity of the benefits system. Housing wealth can provide many benefits, and be spent on many things, but it cannot do everything. For too long, its potential has been overstated.

Introduction

How should the Government respond to the increasing importance of housing wealth? An investment and a consumption good, a source of security and a focus of aspirations, net housing wealth accounted for just over 50 per cent of identified personal wealth in 2004 (HM Revenue and Customs 2006b). It is also deeply political, jostled by debates on aspirations, pensioner poverty, care needs and inheritance. But what should the strategic goals of government policy with respect to housing wealth be, and how can they be best achieved?

Two problems stand out. First, house prices have increasingly taken homeownership out of reach of young, first-time buyers, redistributing wealth from renters to owners. How much does this matter? Is housing wealth different from other forms of wealth, in the way it feeds inequality, affects the behaviour of owners, or changes communities? And does this mean that government should support homeownership?

Second, older pensioners are increasingly attempting to square housing wealth with income poverty. As the number of homeowning pensioners rises, and the adequacy of pensions falls, the problem will worsen. Does this mean that government should help pensioners liquidise their housing wealth? Should it re-evaluate the way that housing is (and in some cases, is not) included in means tests?

Linking the two is the question of what, if anything, makes housing different from other forms of wealth, and how important these differences are for different policy objectives.

Section 1 considers housing wealth in the context of access to homeownership. Chapter 1 outlines the policy context, and the Government's stated objectives around increasing access to homeownership. Because our interest is in housing wealth, we focus on two objectives: greater wealth equality and mixed communities, which depend on specific arguments about the nature and effects of housing wealth.

In Chapter 2, we consider wealth accumulation in more detail. Why does the distribution of housing wealth matter? And, if it does, is encouraging or subsidising low earners to invest in housing the most appropriate intervention? Homeownership does appear to lead to wealth accumulation, particularly for those on lower incomes, but this depends on mortgaged housing equity amplifying the benefits and risks. The Government's targets on affordability, if successful, are likely to mean that housing will be a loss-making investment for those on low incomes.

Chapter 3 focuses on whether housing wealth changes attitudes or behaviour, and whether these can be observed at a community level. The evidence on community benefits is not reliable enough to support government subsidies; so, although mixed income neighbourhoods may be desirable, this should not mean focusing subsidies on homeownership.

Section 2 looks at accessing housing wealth later in life. Chapter 4 considers the political and social drivers of demand for releasing housing wealth, which suggest that housing wealth is becoming increasingly important. It looks at the number of asset-rich, income-poor pensioners, and predicted trends in homeownership and demographics.

The next four chapters consider factors that limit the release of housing wealth. The different ways of releasing housing wealth, and their different costs and advantages, are outlined in Chapter 5. It observes that releasing housing wealth is expensive, but that this does not justify government subsidy, which would distort saving from pensions into homes. Chapter 6 considers the attitudes of the current generation of asset-rich, income-poor pensioners towards equity release products and trading down. In focus groups for this project we found that attitudes were negative and deeply held.

Chapters 7 and 8 look at two areas where government does have a clearly defined role. Chapter 7 looks at the interaction with the benefits system, particularly through means testing and the resulting complexity. The disincentive to draw on private resources in retirement adds to already strong arguments in favour of abolishing Pension Credit and replacing it with a non-means-tested British State Pension at the guarantee level of Pension Credit.

Chapter 8 considers the lack of good quality, affordable financial advice and the role of government in improving both product-specific and generic provision.

Chapter 9 focuses on trading down as a means of releasing housing wealth. Those who would like to trade down are prevented from doing so, in particular, by a lack of suitable housing to move into, and, for older pensioners, the logistical process of the move itself.

Chapter 10 offers some conclusions, drawing together policy recommendations and directions for future research.

Access to homeownership

1. The policy context

In this chapter:
- We argue that government support for homeownership is often justified in terms of people's aspirations to become homeowners, but aspirations are not enough.
- We show that some arguments for supporting homeownership are based on it being the most cost-effective way of helping those in housing need. Other arguments rely on the unique benefits of homeownership as distinct from other tenures and forms, and these are the focus of our report.

A growing consensus is forming that government should support homeownership. It is most succinctly expressed by the Conservative party's statement of values, voted on by party members in February 2006:

> We believe in the role of government as a force for good. It can and should support aspirations such as home ownership, saving for a pension, and starting a business.

Conservative Party 2006

Meanwhile, in the run-up to the 2005 general election, Gordon Brown announced his intention to create a further one million homeowners (Brown 2005). Supporting the expansion of homeownership is expensive: the 2006 Budget announced £970 million for shared equity schemes (Brown 2006), and, at a cost of £40 million, increased the tax-free allowance of stamp duty. This came on top of a £250 million cost from doubling the allowance to £120,000 in 2004-05, justified largely in terms of helping first-time buyers.

Section 106 agreements, through which developers compensate local authorities for the costs of development, are also used to provide low-cost homeownership. And reimbursing housing associations for discounts given under the HomeBuy shared ownership proposals is expected to cost £30 million a year (Office of the Deputy Prime Minister [ODPM] 2005a). More details of the policies to support homeownership are given in Box 1.1, opposite.

Why should homeownership be supported? People's aspirations to own their own home play a part. But aspirations are not enough, as can be illustrated by replacing one aspiration with another. If you would prefer to own a Honda than a home, does that mean that government should support you

Box 1.1: Current government policies to promote homeownership

Right to buy
Most council tenants who have lived in their property for at least two years (or five for those who have taken up tenancy after 18 January 2005) have the right to buy the home they are living in at a discount. The discount offered on the purchase of homes starts at 32 per cent of market value for houses, and rises by one per cent each year to a maximum of 60 per cent. For flats, the maximum starts at 44 per cent, and rises two per cent each year to a maximum of 70 per cent. The discount was capped at £16,000 in many parts of the South East in 2003.

Right to acquire
Tenants of social landlords or housing associations who have lived in their home for at least two years (or five for those whose tenancy began after 18 January 2005) can buy their home at a discount of £9,000–£16,000.

HomeBuy
The cost of homes, as well as any future price increases, are shared between individuals and housing associations. Introduced in April 2006, this replaced and rationalised Shared Ownership, HomeBuy and the First Time Buyers Initiative, all of which allowed some form of shared ownership. There are three types:

Social HomeBuy: Enables existing social tenants to purchase a share of the equity in an existing housing association or local authority home. They can purchase between 25 and 75 per cent. The landlord can levy a rent of up to three per cent of the remaining equity.

New Build HomeBuy: Social tenants, those on the housing register, key workers and first-time buyers who have been identified and prioritised for assistance by the Regional Housing Board will be eligible. The same terms and conditions on equity shares and rent apply as for Social HomeBuy. The First Time Buyer's Initiative for homes built on public land will be subsumed into New Build HomeBuy.

Open Market HomeBuy: Eligibility is the same as for New Build HomeBuy. Individuals can buy at least 75 per cent of a property on the open market, with the rest bought by a housing association.

Key worker living
Equity loans of up to £50,000 or £100,000 are available to help key workers,

cont. next page

such as nurses and teachers, in order to help them to buy their own property. From April 2006, eligibility is expanding to include all NHS clinical staff (excluding doctors and dentists); teachers in schools, further education and sixth form colleges; police officers and community support officers; uniformed staff in fire and rescue services; prison and probation staff; social workers, occupational therapists, educational psychologists, rehabilitation officers for the visually impaired, speech and language therapists and qualified nursery nurses; local-authority-employed clinical staff and local authority planners.

Voluntary Purchase Grant Scheme
Enables housing association tenants who do not qualify for Right to Acquire to buy their home at a discount of £9,000-£16,000. The scheme is voluntary and housing associations may decide to opt in or out.

Cash incentive scheme
Payment of a grant to local authority tenants to assist them in buying a property in the private sector. Local authorities can decide whether or not to run a CIS scheme.

Stamp duty exemption
No stamp duty is paid on homes worth less than £125,000. Homes worth £125,001-£250,000 are taxed at one per cent; £250,001-£500,000 at three per cent; and above that at four per cent (2006-7).

Capital gains tax exemption
Capital gains tax is not paid on the main or only home. This is only partly about encouraging homeownership; it is also an acknowledgement that homeowners who wish to move house will require their capital gains to purchase a property of equivalent value.

in your purchase? Rather, government support for owning a home needs to be justified with reference to specific social considerations, which might include social justice, community benefits, citizenship, or market failures. Even intervention on these grounds will have resource implications that must be weighed against other objectives and policy instruments.

In the case of housing, ippr's Commission on Sustainable Development in the South East (Commission on Sustainable Development in the South East 2005) identified eight different objectives for investment in housing, all requiring resources. One pound spent on low-cost homeownership may mean one pound less for improving the standard of the existing housing stock, reducing homelessness, or addressing low housing demand in areas of the north.[1]

The Government gave its own reasons for supporting homeownership in a 2005 consultation on HomeBuy (see also HM Treasury and ODPM 2005, 2005a), and it is in the context of these that this reports looks at housing wealth. The objectives given by the Government were:

1. *Creating mixed, sustainable communities:* enabling people to buy their home can create a better balance of housing types and tenures, and a mix of incomes, for instance if it encourages people on higher incomes to stay in predominantly social rented areas. This can help to promote more sustainable communities and to tackle concentrations of deprivation, which have a negative impact on people's life chances.

2. *Achieving value for money:* home ownership can be an appropriate and cost effective means of helping people in housing need, both from the perspective of the individual and from that of the Government.

3. *Freeing up social housing:* if people move out of a social rented home to take up a home ownership opportunity, this frees up social homes for households in greater housing need, such as households living in temporary accommodation.

4. *Increasing overall supply:* if a home ownership subsidy is used to build a new home, or if receipts from the sale of existing homes are ploughed back into new housing, this increases the overall supply of housing, helping to ease the upward pressures on house prices.

5. *Aiding recruitment and retention of key workers:* in areas of high demand for housing, providing assistance for key workers in the public sector to buy a home near to their place of work can help to address recruitment and retention difficulties.

6. *Enabling more people to share in increasing asset wealth:* homes are not just places to live. They are also assets – assets which now account for over 40 per cent of wealth, compared to just over 20 per cent in 1971. But this increase in wealth is unevenly spread. Support for home ownership will enable more people on lower incomes to benefit from any further increases in the value of housing assets.

ODPM 2005a: 7

Two of these objectives are almost identical, and deserve support: 'achieving value for money' and 'freeing up social housing' suggest that home-

---

1. Other objectives were: increasing the rate of build of social housing; more low-cost home-ownership; reforming rents and Housing Benefit; and improving affordability.

ownership policies are simply another way of meeting housing need. Both suggest that households should be able to cash in future entitlement to social housing, and spend the money getting into homeownership. Specific policies have to show that value for money is, in fact, achieved, so that helping people into homeownership costs less than the net present value of providing equivalent social housing, taking into account all direct and indirect subsidies. But expectations are that this will indeed be the case for HomeBuy (Bramley *et al* 2002, ODPM 2005e, 2005g).

Two of the objectives are questionable, but should be decided by a close evaluation of specific policies, which lies outside the scope of this book. Whether the objective to 'increase overall supply' should be pursued through homeownership, rather than alternative means, depends on the economics of specific policies. As pointed out by the Commission on Sustainable Development in the South East (2005), the total drop in new housing since the mid-1960s is clearly attributable to a reduction in the number of social houses built, rather than the number of houses available for homeownership. Similarly, 'the recruitment and retention of key workers' is an unsurprising objective in itself, but may be better achieved through other means. The Government needs to refute criticisms about unclear targeting. In some schemes, such as Key Worker Living, workers who benefit receive very large amounts of help, including equity loans of up to £100,000, while others receive nothing. Those who receive support are not necessarily poor, with an average income of £33,000 (ODPM 2005a: 17).

The two remaining objectives relate directly to the nature of housing wealth, so are examined in more detail in this report. 'Enabling more people to share in increasing asset wealth' and achieving 'mixed and sustainable communities' are important objectives. The question for this report is whether homeownership is the best way of achieving them – and answering this involves a more detailed examination of how housing wealth is acquired, and how (if at all) owning housing wealth affects behaviour.

To unpick the thinking behind these objectives, Chapter 2 looks at housing wealth as an asset. Why is the distribution of housing wealth a concern for government? And, if it is, is it best addressed through housing wealth itself, by encouraging individuals to invest in it, or through other channels? Is housing, in fact, a good investment for those on low incomes?

Chapter 3 looks at how housing wealth may change behaviour or attitudes. Does owning housing wealth lead to a change in incentives or patterns of thought? Does it, for example, create an 'asset effect', in increased security, autonomy and propensity to plan? Can this be traced to positive outcomes at the neighbourhood level? And, if so, does this mean that 'mixed communities' should be achieved directly through mixed tenure, or is tenure merely a symptom of the types of 'mix' that matter?

2. Wealth accumulation

This chapter argues:

- The housing market has been a self-reinforcing driver of wealth inequality. Acquiring housing wealth has increasingly required wealth, so that those without access to family resources are excluded.

- Those with some wealth have tended to acquire more. An American study found that, after 15 years of homeownership, low-income homeowners were 14 times wealthier than equivalent renters.

- But, although housing has fed wealth inequality, we must look elsewhere for the solution. Housing cannot deliver wealth to all. This becomes clear when looking at the factors that make homeownership profitable. House price increases are paid for by non-owners, and are unearned; leveraging investment in the home through a mortgage magnifies losses as well as gains, is less suitable for those less able to manage the risks and will become less profitable as house price growth falls; and a pre-commitment to save is riskier for those on low incomes, who tend to have more volatile incomes and less robust coping mechanisms.

Therefore the Government should:

- challenge the distribution of windfall gains to housing wealth, using the introduction of planning-gain supplement to create political space

- use the charged issue of homeownership to add new priority to regional policy, as a way of helping to slow house price rises, and prevent the further redistribution of wealth from non-owners to owners

- build public support for its affordability targets early, as they will create losers.

The housing market has fed wealth inequality

Increasing house prices have contributed to increasing wealth inequality in the UK. Michael Heseltine, speaking as Environment Minister when the first Right to Buy legislation was passing into law, said:

> I believe that, in a way and on a scale that was quite unpredictable, ownership of property has brought financial gain of immense value to millions of our citizens … [but] this dramatic change in property values has opened up a division in the nation between those who own their homes and those who do not.

Heseltine 1979

If he was concerned then, he should be panicked now. By 2004, over 2.3 million households had entered homeownership through the Right to Buy policy (Wilcox 2005), but house price inflation has put homeownership even further out of reach of others. Inequality of wealth is in danger of becoming self-sustaining: acquiring housing wealth has required wealth, and those who own some have gained more.

Housing inequality is part of a broader picture of high wealth inequality. The wealthiest one per cent owned almost a quarter of all the wealth in the country in 2003, while almost a third of the population had marketable wealth of less than £5,000 (HM Revenue and Customs 2006a). The gini coefficient for wealth inequality is twice as high as for income inequality, at 0.7 compared to 0.35 (HM Revenue and Customs 2006a: Table 13.5). And wealth inequality has been growing over the past 20 years: the number of households without any assets doubled from five to 10 per cent between 1979 and 1996 (Paxton 2002), and, in the late 1990s, the top one per cent increased their wealth share by around three percentage points.

Acquiring housing wealth requires wealth

Fast-increasing house prices in some areas of the country are shutting many out of the market. The Low Cost Homeownership Taskforce (2003) identified an affordability gap, a savings gap and an information gap as barriers to homeownership. To a large extent, the savings gap and the monthly income requirement are substitutes, as a larger deposit reduces the monthly cost of a mortgage. An increasing house-price-to-income ratio raises both the wealth and income requirements, but only some people are able to circumvent them by calling on family resources.

As long as house price growth is higher than income growth, an individual's ability to buy a house becomes increasingly determined by parental wealth – and, in particular, whether, when and where their parents and grandparents bought a house.

Research from the Council of Mortgage Lenders (CML) shows that help with a deposit is increasingly important for first-time buyers (Tatch 2006). By looking at how much could have been plausibly saved by individuals under 30 in their working life to date, and comparing that to their deposit, Tatch divides first-time buyers into the 'assisted' and 'unassisted'. The number of unassisted first-time buyers under 30 fell by three quarters between 1995 and 2005, from 140,000 to 33,000, while the number who were assisted more than doubled, from 11,000 in 1995 to 26,000 in 2004, before falling back to 15,000 in 2005 (see Figure 2.1). Some of these movements are likely to be cyclical, as the period in question covers only the upswing of the housing cycle from the trough in 1995.

These findings are confirmed by other studies. The Office of the Deputy Prime Minister (ODPM) found that over a third of first-time buyers

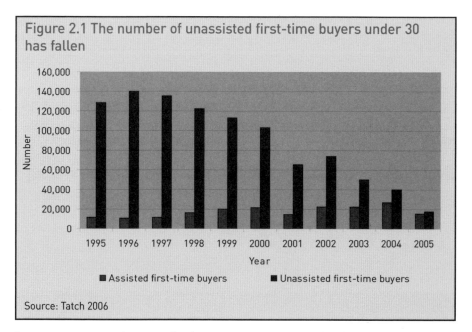

Figure 2.1 The number of unassisted first-time buyers under 30 has fallen

Number

160,000
140,000
120,000
100,000
80,000
60,000
40,000
20,000
0

1995 1996 1997 1998 1999 2000 2001 2002 2003 2004 2005

Year

■ Assisted first-time buyers   ■ Unassisted first-time buyers

Source: Tatch 2006

between 1995 and 2001 relied to some extent on gifts, family loans, inheritance or windfall (quoting ODPM 2005h, Barker 2003: Table 1.4).

Owning housing wealth delivers wealth

Historically, the real returns from investing in housing have been relatively strong. In Britain, the mean annualised real rate of return on housing, over 20-year periods from 1930 to 2003, was 5.6 per cent. This figure is adjusted for actual and implicit rents and the cost of maintenance, and is slightly lower than the 6.4 per cent on equities (Pensions Commission 2004). Although housing wealth is rarely diversified, usually being invested in a single asset, housing as a category is relatively stable compared to other investment options. House price growth has been particularly fast in the most recent cycle, as shown by Figure 2.2 (next page).

Partly as a result of house price rises, studies that track renters and owners show that owners tend to end up much wealthier. In an American study using the Panel Study of Income Dynamics, Di *et al* (2003) showed that there was a large difference in net wealth in 1999 between those who had been renting in 1984 and those who had owned their own home. This controlled for a wide range of other characteristics, including income at different points, although it is not possible entirely to exclude the possibility of self-selection effects. Other datasets provide supporting evidence, although their findings are less robust (for example, Di 2003).

Homeowners on low incomes tend to earn lower returns, but homeownership is more important for them as a way of accumulating wealth. Trends in house prices have been less favourable in poorer areas in the UK,

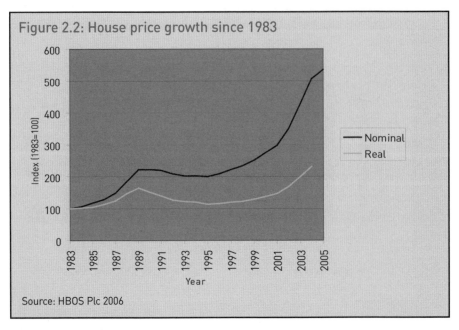

Figure 2.2: House price growth since 1983

Index (1983=100)

Year

Nominal
Real

Source: HBOS Plc 2006

so that, over the period 1983-2003, the percentage increase in property values in the most expensive tenth of areas was almost twice that for the least expensive tenth in the UK (Thomas and Dorling 2004).

At the same time, a longitudinal study of renters and owners in the US showed that the difference in wealth between renters and owners was actually more pronounced for those on low incomes (Di *et al* 2003). The study controlled for demographic factors, income and initial wealth, and found that low-income homeowners who owned for all 15 years of the study were, on average, 14 times wealthier than renters with similar characteristics in 1984, whereas non-low-income owners were only five times wealthier than equivalent renters.

The length of ownership was more important for low-income owners than other owners. This may partly be because the fixed costs represent a bigger proportion of the house value – and the moving costs are significant. A survey of first-time buyers by Alliance and Leicester (2005) put the average price of moving at almost £3,000, including stamp duty, land registry fee, survey costs, solicitor fees and removal fees. Adding the cost of furniture and other home essentials increased this figure to £14,000.

Because acquiring housing wealth requires wealth, and owning it delivers more, housing has contributed to a self-reinforcing cycle of inequality. It has transmitted disadvantage from one generation to the next, and, to the extent that society cares about equal opportunities, this should be of deep concern.

Yet a concern for the distribution of housing wealth does not necessarily mean that the solution involves wider homeownership, as the following section shows.

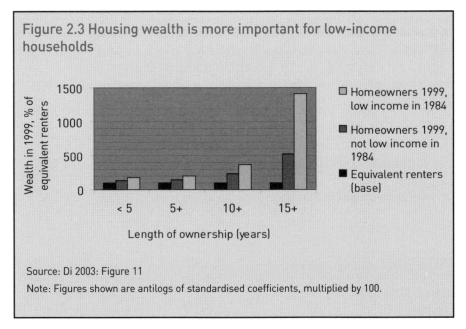

Figure 2.3 Housing wealth is more important for low-income households

- □ Homeowners 1999, low income in 1984
- ■ Homeowners 1999, not low income in 1984
- ■ Equivalent renters (base)

Length of ownership (years): < 5, 5+, 10+, 15+

Y-axis: Wealth in 1999, % of equivalent renters (0, 500, 1000, 1500)

Source: Di 2003: Figure 11

Note: Figures shown are antilogs of standardised coefficients, multiplied by 100.

But housing wealth is not the solution

Money spent on rent is often referred to as 'dead money' by those keen to become owners. Owning, in contrast, is seen as a way of accumulating wealth. But the comparison is not so simple. Homeownership allows a household to increase its wealth by paying off a mortgage and gaining from price increases. But, in the interest repayments, it requires expenditure that is just as 'dead' as money spent on rent. An element of the rent can also be seen as insurance for maintenance and repairs.

So, having observed that housing has delivered wealth to many, we cannot conclude that it could deliver wealth to all. This is revealed more clearly below, by decomposing the key factors that have made housing an effective way to build wealth.

The first, house price inflation, simply redistributes wealth from non-owners to owners. It is an unearned windfall – and, as the previous price increases have been partly caused by a one-off adjustment to low inflation, cannot be expected to continue indefinitely. The second, the fact that mortgaged investments amplify losses and gains on the original capital, makes housing wealth more risky as house price growth slows, particularly for those on low incomes. Finally, the fact that a mortgage forces monthly savings makes them a valuable pre-commitment mechanism, but one that is less suitable for those with less secure incomes.

House price increases are unearned, and paid for by non-owners

House price gains come directly at the expense of non-owners, who find it harder to buy a home of their own and must pay more in rent.

House price gains are largely unearned. It is the value of land, not of buildings or an increase in quality, that has made housing so much more expensive, and this has not come as a result of any action by landowners. Estate agents implicitly recognise this point when they say the key factors are 'location, location, location'. Winston Churchill made the same point in 1909:

> Roads are made, streets are made, services are improved, electric light turns night into day, water is brought from reservoirs a hundred miles off in the mountains – and all the while the landlord sits still... He renders no service to the community, he contributes nothing to the general welfare, he contributes nothing to the process from which his own enrichment is derived.
>
> Barker 2003

Economically and philosophically, a fair solution would be an annual tax on land value (excluding the value of any buildings on top of it) (McLean 2005). This could be levied at, say, half of one per cent, and replace existing property taxes, stamp duty and Council Tax. But, politically, it would be implausibly courageous, as those who would pay more tax are concentrated in marginal constituencies in the South East (Brooks 2005).

Although a full land-value tax remains a distant prospect at best, there are actions that the Government can take now. It is currently in the process of establishing a new planning-gain supplement, a surcharge on developers when they receive a windfall from a change in planning permission (HM Treasury 2005b). Depending on how it is framed and discussed, this could be used as a 'wedge' to open political space and strengthen public understanding of the nature of land value. Whether successful reform opens the way to more ambitious changes, or closes it off, depends, in part, on the arguments and language that are used to support it (see Lakoff 2004).

Similarly, when facing criticisms of stamp duty or inheritance tax, the Government and others could make clear that the increase in yield is largely due to the large windfall gain from housing. The winners are not always those who pay these taxes, but taxes that fall mainly on property are a fair way of paying for the measures needed to ameliorate the effects of house price inflation. Those who have suffered include people shut out of the housing market, and those left homeless or in temporary accommodation as a result of housing shortages.

The negative consequences of increasing house price inflation also add urgency to the Government's desire to reduce it. The Barker Review (Barker 2004) called for a national target of house price affordability, and the Treasury's response (HM Treasury 2005a) accepted the need for regional affordability targets to play a key role in house building – although, as yet, there is no clear indication how these targets might be reached. Previous research by ippr has shown that plausible levels of house building in the

South East are unlikely to be able to meet demand. *All* of the planned increase in building in the South East will be required to meet the backlog of social housing (Commission on Sustainable Development in the South East 2005).

In the long run, addressing damagingly high house price inflation must mean increasing the priority of regional policy. HM Treasury, the Department for Trade and Industry, and the Office of the Deputy Prime Minister currently share a public service agreement to 'reduce the persistent gap in growth rates between the regions' (ODPM 2005f: 8). Other research by ippr has shown that there is more the Government can do to address the regional unbalance of demand (Adams *et al* 2003, Adams and Reed 2006 forthcoming), by making housing supply and demand a more explicit part of decisions that affect the regions, including infrastructure, industrial support and policies to encourage entrepreneurship.

The Government and others could use the issue of access to homeownership as a way of increasing the priority that regional policy is given by the public. Homeownership and house prices are seen as newsworthy and of interest to a wide range of people; regional policy is not. The Government and other stakeholders must communicate the fact that these are interdependent, and that policies to improve the relative economic performance of those regions currently lagging would benefit would-be buyers in more expensive areas.

Leverage magnifies losses as well as gains, and will become less attractive
The second reason that housing wealth has tended to be profitable is that it is typically highly 'leveraged'; that is, the debt-to-equity ratio is typically high. This means that both the gains and losses that result from changes in house prices are very high compared to the sum invested (see Box 2.1, next page). Tracking renters and homeowners from 1984 to 1999, using the American Panel Study of Income Dynamics, Di *et al* (2003) found that buying a more expensive house was associated with owning greater net wealth independently of the amount actually owned. In fact, buying a house in 1984 that was one per cent more expensive was associated with owning 34 per cent more wealth in 1999, controlling for demographic characteristics, income in 1984, 1989, 1994 and 1990, and wealth in 1984.

However, the leverage effect is less profitable, or even loss-making, in a climate of stable or falling house prices. Losses are more likely to occur in the longer term. If targets on affordability are met (Barker 2004, HM Treasury 2005a), a trade-off becomes unavoidable. Either house prices can fall relative to incomes, in which case more people will be able to afford a home but existing homeowners will lose out, or house prices will continue to deliver windfalls to existing homeowners (including those on low incomes), but the remainder will find it even harder to buy their own home.

Box 2.1: Leverage

A simplified illustration of leverage is given below. The effects can work both ways, so that, in the example below, a fall in value of 10 per cent would destroy all the equity owned by the homeowner, and leave an additional debt of £4,500 to pay the mortgage.

	House: leveraged	Equities: not leveraged
Original investment	£10,000	£10,000
Mortgage	£90,000	-
Total value of asset	£100,000	£10,000
Increase in value of 10%	£10,000	£1,000
Gross profit on original investment	£10,000	£1,000
	(100%)	(10%)
Less cost of mortgage (5%)	£4,500	-
Net profit on investment	**£5,500**	**£1,000**
	(55%)	**(10%)**

More generally, it is profitable to invest in leveraged housing if the house price grows by more than the debt. This can be seen most clearly by writing the profit at the end of the period as:

$$\text{Profit from homeownership} = r_h H - r_m(H - I)$$
$$\text{Profit from equities} = r_e I$$

Where r_h and r_e refer to the rates of return on housing and equities respectively, r_m is the rate of interest on mortgages, H is the purchase value of the house, and I is the amount available to invest.

If the rate of return on housing is the same as equities, so $r_h = r_e$, then it is more profitable to invest in housing if $r_{h,e} > r_m$.

This illustration looks only at the effect of leverage on the investment decision. It does not include other important factors that would be included in the decision as a whole, such as the role of housing as a consumption good, rental streams, maintenance and transaction costs, tax treatment and the rate of time preference. It is also possible to leverage equities, for example by purchasing options to buy in the future at a certain price.

A key threshold is whether the rate of growth of house prices is above the rate of mortgage interest, currently around six per cent. Once the growth rate falls below that level, any mortgaged equity will start to cost money rather than provide a profit. Whether this extra cost outweighs the money that must be spent on rent is a more complicated question, which must also take into account the amount that is spent on maintenance, frequency and costs of moving, and individual levels of risk aversion.

The only way to achieve both profitable leverage and improved afford-ability would be if income growth exceeded mortgage rates. This is unlikely, not least because the resulting inflation from income growth would prob-ably result in the Bank of England increasing interest rates.

For example, for affordability to have increased over the last five years, house price growth would have had to have been less than the average income growth of 5.2 per cent (income growth of the second poorest 20 per cent, a key factor for affordability, was somewhat higher, at 5.9 per cent) (Department for Work and Pensions 2005a). At the same time, for leverage to be profitable rather than loss-making, houses prices would had to have grown by *more* than the mortgage rates, which, for building soci-eties, averaged 5.3 per cent over the period (Council of Mortgage Lenders 2006). This is illustrated in Figure 2.4, below.

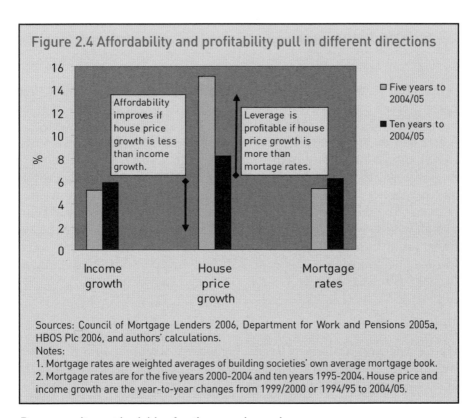

Figure 2.4 Affordability and profitability pull in different directions

Sources: Council of Mortgage Lenders 2006, Department for Work and Pensions 2005a, HBOS Plc 2006, and authors' calculations.
Notes:
1. Mortgage rates are weighted averages of building societies' own average mortgage book.
2. Mortgage rates are for the five years 2000-2004 and ten years 1995-2004. House price and income growth are the year-to-year changes from 1999/2000 or 1994/95 to 2004/05.

Pre-commitment is riskier for those on lower incomes

The third reason that homeownership tends to lead to wealth accumula-tion is that it commits households to saving every month. Part of the mort-gage payment can be seen as paying the cost of the loan, but the amount that reduces net real debt is equivalent to saving. Because individuals have limited self-control, they may prefer a certain degree of inflexibility to help maintain regular saving (Frederick *et al* 2002, Sunstein and Thaler 2003).

Saving pre-commitment can bring substantial risks for those on low incomes as lower incomes tend to be more variable. Analysis of working-age adults in the British Household Panel Survey showed that, for those on low incomes (60-80 per cent of the median), the probability of falling into poverty in the next year was 21 per cent, compared to 1.5 per cent for those with an income greater than 150 per cent of the median (Cappellari and Jenkins 2003, see also Hills *et al* 2006, Meyer *et al* 1994). Doling and Stafford (1989) examined homeownership in Coventry and found that higher income instabilities among low earners meant that they were more likely to experience repossession.

Ford and Quilgars (2001) also found that low-income homeowners who had mortgage payment protection insurance were less successful in bringing a claim than higher-income borrowers. Additionally, state insurance for housing costs provides more help to tenants than owners. The Mortgage Interest component of Income Support, for example, pays out only after 29 weeks on Income Support, pays at a standard interest rate only one percentage point above the Bank of England base rate, and only on capital up to £100,000. This threshold has remained unchanged since 1995.

As more unstable incomes lead to a higher chance of forced sales, they make it much more likely that the sale will be badly timed in the cycle, as happened in the early 1990s. Looking further back, those who invested in housing in the UK in 1973 and who sold in 1977 would have seen a real loss of at least 40 per cent of their capital, before leverage (Farlow 2004).

Any policy to increase access to homeownership would need to encourage *sustainable, affordable* homeownership. Mortgage protection programmes, pre-purchase information and advice are therefore crucial complements to any homeownership promotion programme. A decent asset buffer (aside from the deposit) is a prerequisite to a house purchase, so that low-income homeowners can cope with both income volatility and unpredictable maintenance costs.

Conclusions

Homeownership has driven wealth inequality. Acquiring wealth requires wealth, and owning wealth delivers more. The housing market has been, in at least one sense, biblical:

> For unto every one that hath shall be given, and he shall have abundance: but from him that hath not shall be taken away even that which he hath.

King James Bible, Matthew 25:29

The returns to homeownership tend to be lower for low-income households, but there is some evidence that homeownership plays a more important role in asset building. An American study found that low-income homeowners who owned for all 15 years of the survey were, on average, 14 times wealthier than renters with similar characteristics at the start of the period.

Although the housing market has helped to create wealth for many, it cannot create wealth for all. The best response to housing-driven wealth inequality is not to promote further homeownership. This becomes clear when the drivers of housing profitability are examined: house price rises are unearned by landowners, and are paid for by non-owners; the leverage effect of mortgage-financed homeownership magnifies losses as well as gains so will become less attractive as house price growth falls; and a precommitment to save is riskier for those on low incomes, who tend to have more volatile incomes and less robust coping mechanisms.

To ensure that further house price growth, which will lead to even more redistribution of wealth from non-owners to owners, does not go unchallenged, the Government should:

- make a strong argument that recent house price gains have created losers as well as winners, and that the widely criticised taxation of housing wealth through stamp duty and inheritance tax is a way of paying for measures to address this. The losers from house price increases include those shut out of the housing market, and those left homeless or in temporary accommodation as a result of housing shortages.
- use a framework that stresses the socially created nature of land value when making its case for planning-gain supplement. This would help open political space for new thinking on the treatment of land value.
- ensure that the windfall nature of house price rises is fully understood ahead of any losses (or market corrections).

In the longer term, lower house price growth requires successful action on the regional balance of demand. The Government should:

- use the issue of homeownership to increase the public priority of regional policy. Access to homeownership is newsworthy and of interest to a wide range of people; regional policy is not. The Government and other stakeholders must communicate the fact that these are interdependent issues.

Other research by ippr explored the different ways of putting housing supply and demand centre stage in decisions around regional policy, including infrastructure, industrial support and encouraging entrepreneurship (Adams *et al* 2003, Adams and Reed 2006 forthcoming).

Policies on housing supply and demand will take place in the context of affordability targets, which the Government has provisionally agreed to implement, but has not yet clarified. Meeting the affordability targets, if that can be achieved, will mean that housing will cease to be as attractive an investment. Once house price growth falls below the rate of mortgage interest, the mortgage can no longer be paid by capital gains. If the Government expects the targets to be met, it should therefore:

- Refrain from encouraging people to take out large mortgages, or to think of homeownership as primarily an asset-building strategy.
- Build public support early for affordability targets. They will create losers.

3. Wealth effects: do homeowners think or behave differently?

This chapter looks at the effects that housing wealth has on individuals and communities. It finds:

- There is a developing literature that suggests assets positively affect capabilities, behaviour and attitudes. However, many of these benefits, such as security and propensity to plan, appear to flow more from smaller-scale financial assets than from housing wealth.
- Homeownership does appear to increase the amount of control an individual has over his or her environment, and this tends to be seen as an important attraction of homeownership.
- Some have suggested there are community-level benefits from homeownership, and have posited that these benefits come about through two mechanisms. But the first causal mechanism, residential stability, appears to have negative consequences, particularly for labour mobility, and is of much smaller magnitude when comparing homeownership to social tenancy than to private renting. The second causal mechanism, giving homeowners a stake in property prices, is not supported by the evidence as a motivating factor.
- In terms of the outcomes, political participation appears to increase in areas with high levels of homeownership, but the evidence base relies too heavily on the US, and informal community links appear stronger for renters. Educational attainment is higher in areas with high levels of homeownership, but the direction of causation is highly uncertain. Property upkeep is a promising area, but depends heavily on households having the financial resources to maintain their home.

These arguments, combined with the findings of Chapter 2, suggest that the Government should:

- prioritise an assets ladder rather than a housing ladder. This partly means ensuring that those on low incomes have decent incentives to save.
- be cautious about the extent to which 'mixed communities' can be equated with 'mixed tenure'. The former might entail the latter, but targeting mixed tenure alone will not achieve the desirable characteristics of mixed communities.

Sherraden (1991) argued that asset holding alters people's 'cognitive schemata', mental structures that help frame attitudes to future orientation, stakeholding and autonomy (see also Blum and Kingston 1984). This chapter begins by reviewing the literature on asset-based welfare, and considering to what extent homeownership has positive psychological effects. It then looks at whether homeownership affects the community, to see if there are measurable social benefits to homeownership. If so, does this mean that the Government should actively try to ensure that every area has a high level of homeownership? Does this mean that 'mixed communities', in the ways that matter, can be achieved *through* mixed tenure, rather than the other way round?

ippr has been instrumental in putting asset-based welfare on the UK policy agenda, exploring theories that point to the important long-term benefits of asset ownership (the asset effect), the barriers that prevent those on low incomes from acquiring their own assets, and the duty of government to help overcome these barriers (Bynner and Paxton 2001, Kelly and Lissauer 2000, Paxton 2003). Recent policies that have built on this analysis include the Child Trust Fund, which gives all children born from 1 September 2002 their own nest egg, and the Saving Gateway. The Saving Gateway is a matched savings programme for households on low incomes, currently in its second round of pilots. All savings over an 18-month period are matched by the Government, at a rate from 1:1 to 1:5 depending on the area (Kempson *et al* 2005).

Is there an individual 'homeownership effect'?

Shifting attention from cash savings to housing wealth means focusing on a different group of people. With financial assets, the goal is to increase the asset ownership of those with no or very small formal savings. For example, in the first Saving Gateway pilot, half the participants owned less than £10 in savings at the start of the programme, and 26 per cent had no current account (Kempson *et al* 2005). Potential homeowners, while not necessarily 'rich' (Roger Burrows 2003), must have a reasonable asset buffer and a secure income to make homeownership sustainable.

The language used to describe the benefits of ownership must also be different for different forms of asset, in order not to stigmatise non-owners. Tenure is discrete and more likely to be known, whereas financial wealth is continuous and generally private. Many non-homeowners will never be in a position to own. For some, it will not be in their interests to own, especially given the risks that homeownership can bring. Research should be sensitive in the way that findings are discussed and disseminated.

Assets and personal control
Political philosophers have explored the notion of stakeholding as an 'emancipatory strategy', giving each citizen the material independence necessary to achieve freedom from interference (Ackerman and Alstott 1999, Dowding *et al* 2003, Meade 1964, Paxton *et al* 2006, Van Parijs 1995).

The evidence with respect to savings is encouraging. Among low-income participants in the Government's Saving Gateway, many of those who had not previously saved thought that the programme made them feel 'more in control of my own life'. This feeling was concentrated on those who previously had no savings. Participants who had already had some savings, even at a low level, were less likely to say that their sense of control over their own lives increased as a result of the Saving Gateway.

Increased personal control also appears to be an important factor for homeownership. Saunders (1990) relates homeownership to an increased sense of control over one's resources and physical space. A desire to control one's environment also appears to play an important role in housing aspirations. According to a CML survey, 28 per cent of respondents selected 'being able to do what you want with your own home' as one of the rewards of homeownership (Smith 2004a). Similarly, focus groups conducted by Shelter with 65 non-homeowners, drawn from socio-economic groups C2, D and E, concluded, among other things, that 'people want to feel that their home is their own: that they are able to settle there for as long as they want *and make the place feel like a home'*. (Edwards 2005: 20, emphasis added).

Assets for financial security

Assets are also said to improve security – partly as a result of improved control, but also independently. Security and risk tend to be bigger factors in the decision-making of lower-income households: those on low incomes are more likely to suffer from unemployment (Stewart 1999), crime, particularly if they are on incomes under £5,000 (Nicholas *et al* 2005, table 4.01), and unstable incomes due to benefit mispayment (Preston 2005).

At the same time, coping mechanisms are often less robust. There is a lower likelihood of having insurance, shorter budgeting horizons (for those on fortnightly benefits, for example) and, for some, exclusion from affordable credit markets (Regan and Paxton 2003). When income or expenditure shocks occur, they are more likely to have a bigger impact.

Asset ownership can increase the security of individuals, and thereby allow them to take productive risks in other areas of their lives. When participants in asset-building programmes such as the Saving Gateway pilot are asked to evaluate what difference asset ownership has made to their lives, the focus on security is striking (Kempson *et al* 2005).

> It's made life a little more tolerable because I know I've got it, in the back of my mind now, I know I have got that little bit there if I desperately need it. Which I didn't have before... I would have been more worried about any unplanned for expense before. That would have been in the back of my mind all the time... Well now I know

that I've got a bit more money to cover it.

Saving Gateway participant (Kempson *et al* 2005: 69)

To some extent, security can flow from homeownership as well as from financial savings. A survey by the CML found that 37 per cent of respondents listed 'security' as one of the advantages of homeownership (Smith 2004a). Owning a home opens the door to cheap credit that is secured against the equity in the home, making income smoothing or investment in personal development easier and cheaper. On a larger scale, selling the home can provide substantial sums of money, although this would be a drastic step that most would want to avoid. The wealth is there, and although it is comparatively illiquid it may still provide insulation from the worst risks.

The security provided by homeownership, then, is highly contingent. When income is stable, and house prices are not in danger of falling, owning a home increases security. But, when those conditions do not hold, the effect is the opposite.

Assets and a propensity to plan

One effect of greater security and control may be a greater propensity to plan. This is partly as a result of a reduction in the immediacy of budgeting problems: if an income or expenditure shock does occur, an asset buffer allows an individual to spread the problem over a longer time period. Problems become slightly less immediate.

This longer-term thinking may become a habit. Much of this is consistent with standard economic theory, which states that risk aversion decreases with wealth, and the extent to which the future is valued less than the present (the rate of time discounting) is tied closely to risk aversion. It could also be because accumulating wealth demonstrates to the individual that they can improve their situation through their own actions, increasing their sense of control (Bandura 1995, Sherraden 1991).

The effect of financial assets on planning is more established than the effect of housing wealth. Yadama and Sherraden (1996) found that financial savings in 1968 had a statistically significant relationship with people's propensity to plan, measured with a 'horizons index' in 1972, but that the value of owner-occupied houses did not. The amount we can draw from this study is limited by its focus on house values, a continuous variable, rather than tenure type, a discrete category. At least one paper looking at the effect of savings appeared to show a relatively low 'cut-off', above which more does not mean better (Bynner and Paxton 2001).

The responsibilities of homeownership are unrelated to house value. What could matter is the mental adjustment of seeing oneself as a homeowner, or the extra responsibilities that come with homeownership, rather than the price of the home. If so, then we would indeed expect to see no significant relationship between 'horizons' and house value, but a significant relationship *would* emerge if we looked at tenure type, or house values up to a certain point. Trying to establish whether homeownership increases planning is also complicated by the fact that buying a home requires a considerable degree of planning in the first place, and so homeownership might be a symptom rather than a cause of an individual's greater propensity to plan.

Overall, then, the evidence for psycho-social benefits of homeownership, what we might call a 'homeownership effect', is less reliable than the evidence for the financial 'asset effect'. It does appear to allow greater personal control, and this may lead to greater security. But the former, to some extent, and the latter, even more so, depend on homeownership being combined with adequate financial resources. Financial assets must come before housing wealth. The evidence for an increased propensity to plan appears, at this stage, unconvincing.

Does homeownership benefit the community?

There is an ongoing debate about the ways and the extent to which concentrated disadvantage has a negative effect (Atkinson and Kintrea 2001, O'Regan and Quigley 1996, Speak and Graham 1999). Berube (2006) discusses how deprived neighbourhoods may influence several pathways to social mobility, including employment, education, crime and health. After reviewing American and British literature, Gibbons *et al* (2005) conclude that living in a more deprived neighbourhood does have an independent impact for residents. They argue that this effect is most pronounced for crime, more modest for child education, and does not exist for adult employment except in geographically isolated locations.

The question here, though, is whether *tenure* affects outcomes independently of income, education, age, or other characteristics. If so, then creating 'mixed communities' could mean that helping tenants into homeownership should be a policy objective in itself. But, if homeownership is merely a proxy for other characteristics, then artificially turning tenants into homeowners, without affecting who is actually resident in the area, would not bring about these secondary effects. The policy would not necessarily create 'mixed communities' in the ways that matter.

The question can be approached in two ways. We first look at the most frequently cited causal mechanisms, namely, that a stake in local property prices and reduced household mobility lead to greater community and political involvement. The evidence for the first claim is weak, and reduced household mobility comes with significant costs. We then look at the social benefits that homeownership is purported to deliver: improved community involvement, educational attainment and physical upkeep. Statistical studies, mostly in the US, have suggested homeownership leads to positive outcomes in terms of all three, but a question remains about whether these findings apply in the UK.

Reduced mobility brings important costs

Homeowners tend to live longer in one place than private renters, and this may mean that they are more active in their community. Böheim and Taylor (1999) looked at the British Household Panel Study 1991-1997, and found that individuals who lived in the private rented sector were 20 per cent more likely to move than homeowners with a mortgage. Those in local authority rented housing were 3.5 per cent more likely to move. Residential stability does appear to play a large part in explaining the apparent benefits of homeownership. DiPasquale and Glaeser (1999) found that homeownership in the US appeared to contribute to membership of professional organisations – but that 92 per cent of this relationship disappeared when residential stability was taken into account.

Yet residential stability is not an unalloyed good. There is a potential trade-off between low mobility and unemployment. Owner-occupiers appear less likely to move to seek work, pushing up unemployment rates (Green and Hendershott 2001, Oswald 1996, 1997).

Communities that are more stable may also *increase* community tensions. In the ex-coalmining communities in Yorkshire, migration was found to increase a 'social capital index' from 60.9 to 64.6 over the two years to 2002/3 (Green *et al* 2005). Moving within the area, the authors suggest, is often in response to problems with near neighbours, while people leaving the area are often those who are most discontent with it. Reducing mobility through homeownership would reduce people's ability to avoid problem neighbours, and reduce the 'subtraction of malcontents' (Green *et al* 2005: 52), thereby undermining rather than promoting social capital.

Having a stake in local property prices does not necessarily motivate homeowners to be more involved in the community

Aside from duration of residence, the most significant way that homeownership is thought to bring community benefits is by giving people a stake in local property prices, which encourages them to be active in their community or in local politics (Blum and Kingston 1984, Green *et al* 2005, Rohe and Stewart 1996, Saunders 1979, quoted in Rohe *et al* 2000). It is argued that homeowners, by participating in local organisations, are able to ward off threats to their housing equity.

But each homeowner faces a free-rider problem, whereby the costs of effort are individual, but the benefits are shared. There is also evidence that community engagement is not consciously motivated by a desire to protect property values, contrary to the predictions of this theory. Cox (1982) measured 'investment orientation' by asking people how important it was to 'buy houses … so they can sell later at a profit'. People's answers had virtually no relationship to their activism. It should be noted, however, that this study was based on a sample with a relatively small number of observations, and that this finding does not exclude the possibility that motivations are unconsciously or covertly financial.

It is thus not possible to conclude confidently that a stake in local property prices motivates community involvement.

Findings on community involvement and political participation are mixed, and less convincing for the UK than the US

Leaving aside why such relationships might develop, studies from the US do suggest that measures of community and political engagement are higher among homeowners and in home-owning areas. DiPasquale and Glaeser (1999), for example, found that homeowners in the US were six per cent more likely to say they worked to solve local problems, and were, on average, members of 0.25 more non-professional organisations than non-owners, after taking into account a wide range of other factors such as age, marital status, children, income, education, residential structure type (such as semi-detached) and city size. They were also 10 per cent more likely to know their US Representative by name, and 15 per cent more likely to vote.

Similarly, Perkins et al (1990) found that, in the US, a higher proportion of homeowners on a residential block increased block-level participation in the community, based on 48 blocks in an urban area. However, at least one study has suggested that non-homeowners may have more informal community participation. Rossi and Weber (1996) found that renters spent more time socialising with neighbours, co-workers and friends.

Both sets of results appear highly specific to the US, however. The study by DiPasquale and Glaeser (1999) also looked at German data, and, although the relationships between homeownership and citizenship remained statistically significant, the magnitude was much smaller in Germany, dropping by some measures by up to 75 per cent. In Britain the alternative to homeownership is very different to that in the US, and it would be a plausible conjecture that the structure of social housing means that tenants have *more* social capital than owners, not less. At least one analysis in Britain, based on bivariate analysis in three British towns, did indeed find that renters had closer ties to neighbours and were more likely to provide informal aid (Saunders 1990).

So, although correlations from the US are significant, they can be mixed, and have not been shown to exist in the UK. On the basis of current evidence, it is hard to argue that areas with low levels of homeownership would benefit from improved community or political engagement if homeownership levels rose. The case for intervention on this basis may improve after more research, but it is currently weak.

Educational attainment

A British study by Bramley and Karley (2005) found that parental home-ownership is associated with higher levels achievement within their child's school, independently of other factors. The benefits appeared to be greater at the school level than at the individual level, suggesting that homeownership may have 'effects which operate at the school level, such as ethos, expectations, parental involvement, and behaviour' (Bramley and Karley 2005: 23).

Attainment at age 11 was higher in areas with a higher level of owner-occupation: a 20 per cent rise in owner-occupation levels was associated with a rise in mean test scores of 3.5 per cent. The difference was statistically significant after controlling for individual pupil attributes, such as free school meal eligibility; structural characteristics of schools, such as size and spending resources; special policy measures, such as Education Action Zones; and other neighbourhood characteristics, such as a low income index and employment levels.

This is a striking result, although a few notes of caution must be sounded. First, parental *wealth* was not controlled for, which means that it might be parental wealth rather than homeownership that is associated with this effect. Second, although any improvement in school results is welcome, and school-level effects are often small, the study reports a relatively small increase in attainment associated with very large increases in levels of homeownership. Third, we cannot be entirely sure about the direction of causality, which we discuss below.

A US study has suggested that the educational benefits of homeownership might be greatest for low-income families. Green and White (1997) found that homeownership increased the probability of being in school at age 17 by four percentage points when the child's parents were at mean income, but by nine percentage points when they were on low income. The authors confirmed the result against the Public Use Microsample of the 1980 Census of Housing and Population: the effect of 10 years' homeownership was seven percentage points greater for children in low-income than mean-income families (although four years' homeownership did not have the same effect).

But the theory has yet to catch up with the data. Rather than homeownership leading to better schools, better schools may lead to more home-ownership, as wealthier households move into the area and increased demand for homes pushes up house prices in the school catchment area. This is so common in Britain that school quality is reflected in property prices, with a ten percentage point improvement in the school 'league table' at age 11 adding at least three per cent to the price of a house located immediately next it (Gibbons and Machin 2005).

Moving from an average house outside a weak school to a similar house outside a high-performing, oversubscribed school would cost an average of £61,000, based on prices in April-June 2004. More expensive houses also add another feedback mechanism, by changing the class mix of the catchment area.

Much of the benefit also appears to come from associated characteristics, which are not always taken into account. Aaronson (2000), for example, found that homeownership had a positive impact on the likelihood of graduating from high school by the age of 19, but that almost half of this disappeared after controlling for the proportion of years with a move between seven and 16. The model by Bramley and Karley (2005) does take account of housing mobility.

Initially, therefore, the links between homeownership and educational attainment appear positive, but are uncertain foundations on which to base policy. The causal mechanisms that are suggested, such as community participation, a stake in property prices, or reduced mobility, have already been shown to be unreliable.

Homeownership appears to improve physical upkeep, but requires financial resources

Harvard President Lawrence Summers once quipped that 'in the history of the world, no one has ever washed a rented car'. A rational person puts more effort into looking after something he or she owns than something he or she rents, because ownership allows the full benefit of the investment to be reaped. The same appears true of houses (Galster 1983, 1987, Mayer 1981).

Splitting ownership from occupancy brings costs to both sides: the benefit of upkeep is split, so neither side is prepared to invest the full amount; the tenant has less incentive to act on problems early, when they are cheaper to fix; and the landlord must spend additional effort monitoring the behaviour of the tenant. The result is that both may invest less time and effort in property maintenance than is efficient. The 2004 English House Condition Survey found that private rented homes had the worst standard of upkeep, with 42.6 per cent defined as non-decent compared to 26.6 for owner-occupied and 31.3 per cent for the social sector. This does not, though, take age or income into account.

Importantly for public policy, the 'broken window' theory of crime suggests that the state of people's homes could have a wider impact on the neighbourhood. Developed by Wilson and Kelling (1982), this emphasises the signalling function of neighbourhood characteristics. If one window is left broken, passers-by will assume that no one cares about the building, and soon it will have no windows. Those who live and work in the area withdraw as they begin to feel more vulnerable, and become less willing to intervene to maintain public order or to address physical signs of deterioration. The reverse could also be true: a fresh coat of paint on a house, pot plants or a new front door can all give the impression of pride in the local area.

However, property upkeep can only be improved if new buyers have the resources needed to maintain their homes, not, for example, if they became homeowners only because of substantial discounts, and so lack the savings or income that are necessary. Poor maintenance is far from unknown in the owner-occupied sector: a detailed study of house conditions in Wales found that 72 per cent of all unfit dwellings in Wales were in the homeowner sector (Burrows and Wilcox 2004).

For homeownership to increase physical upkeep, then, residents must also have the financial assets to maintain their home.

Conclusions

Homeownership does appear to have some influence on the thinking and behaviour of owners, but this is frequently less than the effect of financial wealth, or only applies if financial wealth is also present. There are also frequent issues with positive findings from the US being of questionable validity in the UK.

In terms of a 'homeownership effect' on individuals, personal control over one's physical space and environment appear to be improved by homeownership. Possibly as a consequence of this, security is viewed as an important benefit of homeownership. This may increase self-efficacy. However, there is no evidence that the propensity to plan is increased by homeownership. The 'homeownership effect' in other respects appears weaker than the 'financial asset effect'.

Links between homeownership and positive community outcomes, meanwhile, have been the subject of some positive and interesting research from the US. But the effects of homeownership on behaviour in the UK cannot be traced through to community benefits in a reliable way. The first causal mechanism, residential stability, may have negative consequences, particularly for labour mobility, and is of much smaller magnitude when comparing homeownership to social tenancy than to private renting. The effect of the second causal mechanism, giving homeowners a stake in property prices, is not supported by the evidence.

In terms of outcomes, political participation appears to be higher in areas with high levels of homeownership, but the evidence base relies too heavily on the US to draw strong conclusions for the UK, and informal community links appear stronger for renters. Educational attainment does appear higher in areas with high levels of homeownership, and this is supported by UK data, but the direction of causation is highly uncertain. Property upkeep is a promising area, but depends heavily on households having the financial resources to maintain their home. When they do not, homeowners are at greater risk of having non-decent homes than renters.

These findings lead to the conclusion that helping individuals to build financial assets should take greater priority than helping them to build housing assets. The psycho-sociological effects of financial assets appear stronger, and the community-level benefits that we might expect from homeownership can only start to accrue when households also have an asset buffer. Financial assets are a pre-condition for successful and sustainable homeownership.

Furthermore, as explored in Chapter 2, some financial wealth is required to become a homeowner. The effects of inequality are more acute further down the distribution, and helping low-to-middle earners to own a home should not come at the expense of helping poorer people to own something. And, as Chapter 5 makes clear, housing wealth is hard to access, so even those who do acquire it may find it hard to make useful.

We should therefore think in terms of a more general asset ladder rather than a housing ladder. The Government should:

- ensure that those on low incomes have decent incentives to save. This could be achieved through a rollout of the Saving Gateway pilots.

What does the preceding analysis imply for HomeBuy, the Government's shared ownership programme? One objective of HomeBuy (and support for homeownership more generally) is value for money. If an individual is expected to receive subsidised housing for a long period of time, it may be cheaper for the Government to give them the upfront support to make them self-sufficient.

Modelling commissioned by the Office of the Deputy Prime Minister (Tribal HCH 2005), suggested that, in most instances, this is the case. Including gains from 'staircasing' (when the individual increases the amount they own), New Build HomeBuy represents a positive net present value if owned for at least five to 10 years, depending on levels of ownership. Excluding gains from staircasing makes a large difference, so that 12 to 29 years are required to achieve a positive net present value. Open Market HomeBuy achieves a positive net present value if owned for at least one to two years including staircasing gains, or one to seven years excluding them.

These findings, though, depend on 23 different assumptions, including income and house price growth, service charges, mortgage rates and different grant levels. As the policy develops, and different variables change, it will be necessary to continue evaluating whether HomeBuy represents good value for money as a way of helping those in housing need. If this ceases to be the case, then it may well be more effective to achieve the other objectives of housing policy – such as mixed communities and equal access to housing wealth – through other means.

What does the analysis mean for the objective of mixed communities? Our analysis prompts scepticism about the view that a desirable mix in communities means a mix of tenure *in itself*. Although we cannot exclude the possibility that an independent effect will emerge after more research, shifting tenants into homeownership could superficially imitate a mixed community, without necessarily bringing about the mixes in incomes, skills and attitudes that are actually important. Our scepticism about mixed tenure as an independent factor does not reduce the importance of mixed communities in the broader sense of mixed-income neighbourhoods.

Even if there are community benefits from homeownership, it is not clear what the *right level* of homeownership may be. Is more always better? Or are there thresholds and tipping points, diminishing marginal returns, or other non-linearities? We might expect that the social benefits of one extra homeowner decline as more people own, while the marginal social benefits of the private rented sector increase (for example, through labour mobility). At some point the lines would cross, and the marginal social benefit of the private rented sector would exceed that of homeownership. Given that, and the current high level of homeownership nationally, it is important to understand the point at which trade-offs start to bite.

Nor is it clear at what level we should understand *community*: should there be a certain proportion of homeowners in each street, each ward, or each local authority? The size at which communities are analysed has important implications for policy, but we are not able to say what that size should be.

This analysis suggests that the Government should:

- continue to ensure that new developments have a mix of tenure, so that those on higher incomes are able to move in.
- exercise caution in how mixed communities are achieved on existing estates. Artificially shifting tenants into homeownership cannot be expected to deliver the benefits of mixed communities: mixed tenure is a consequence, not a cause, of mixed communities. If the concern is retaining those on upward income trajectories, this may be better achieved through site improvements than direct subsidies.

Housing wealth in retirement

4. The social and policy contexts

It is currently a good time to take a strategic overview of housing wealth in later life. It could potentially feed into policy agendas on pensions, care needs, property upkeep and housing supply. This chapter finds:

- One fifth of the retired living in poverty, 440,000 people, own more than £100,000 of housing wealth.
- Housing wealth is likely to be even more important in the future, as levels of homeownership increase and more couples remain childless.
- But there is a danger that housing wealth is overcommitted. Not all the housing wealth owned by asset-rich, income-poor pensioners will, or even can, be released.
- Four factors are constraining the release of housing wealth:
  - It is inherently expensive to release housing wealth, either through equity release or trading down.
  - The current generation of asset-rich, income-poor pensioners have deep-seated objections to equity release.
  - Means-tested benefits are a disincentive for pensioners on benefits to release housing wealth.
  - There is a lack of good quality, affordable financial advice.

We consider the role of government in light of these barriers in Chapters 5 to 8.

The first section of this report argued that the Government should not be encouraging new homeowners to accumulate housing wealth as a means of saving for retirement. But the use of housing wealth in later life by current homeowners is ripe for review.

Historic increases in house prices mean that there is a current generation of homeowners, either approaching or already in retirement, with significant amounts of housing wealth but inadequate pension savings. Releasing wealth from the home, either by selling up and buying a less expensive home, or borrowing against it, could potentially go some way towards filling funding gaps in pensions, domiciliary care needs, and property upkeep. In this chapter we outline the social trends that suggest that housing wealth might be of increasing importance: the increasing number of asset-rich but income-poor pensioners, the high levels of homeownership in the baby boomer generation and increasing numbers of childless pensioners.

What is the role of government in the light of these trends? What does it mean to provide 'the right framework for schemes such as equity release', as the Labour party promised in its 2005 manifesto (Labour Party 2005)? Is the role of government limited to regulation of lifetime mortgages, in place since November 2004, and of home reversion plans, which the Government announced will come under FSA regulation in the future (HM Treasury 2004b)? Or is it a much bigger task? The four chapters that follow look at the some of the major impediments that exist to accessing this wealth: the high cost involved, the negative attitudes of many pensioners to equity release products, the disincentives presented by the benefit system and the lack of financial advice.

Social trends suggest that housing wealth is likely to become more important

One fifth of pensioners living in poverty own more than £100,000 of housing wealth

In a working paper for this project, Sodha (2005) looked into the extent of asset wealth and income poverty among the retired population, using data from the 2002-03 English Longitudinal Study of Ageing (ELSA). She found that a significant number of those who are retired and who live in poverty own a decent amount of housing wealth, and that this figure is likely to increase over the next five to 10 years. These are people who lack adequate retirement income, and who are least likely to have the funds available to maintain their home to a decent standard, or to pay for everyday extras such as domiciliary care.

In fact, around one fifth of those who were retired and living in poverty[2] owned equivalised housing wealth over £100,000 in 2003. This amounts to 4.4 per cent of the overall retired population, or 440,000 retired people[3]. They each owned, on average, £177,000 of housing wealth, £77.1 billion in total.

Similar findings apply for those living just above the poverty threshold. One fifth of retired people had an income above Age Concern's 'Modest but Adequate' threshold of £157 per week in 2002-03 prices, and owned more than £100,000 of equivalised housing wealth in 2003. This threshold

---

2. Living in poverty is defined as living on an income below 60 per cent of the national median income. Twenty-one per cent of pensioners lived under this threshold in 2002/03 Department for Work and Pensions, Households Below Average Income 2003/04 (London: The Stationery Office 2004a). The measure of income in ELSA and FRS is not equivalent, so we use the 21st percentile income level in the 2002-2003 ELSA dataset: £102 per week.

3. We calculated the total number of retired people in the UK as 9.84 million using data from the 2001 England and Wales, Scotland and Northern Ireland censuses. This data necessitated the assumption that all those aged over 75 are retired, in addition to all those aged 75 or under whose economic status is recorded as retired.

has been calculated as the amount needed to provide for a 'healthy lifestyle with the opportunity to play a full part in society... it provides a lifestyle well above the level needed to avoid poverty but well below luxury' (Age Concern 2002: 2). It also coincides with median income in ELSA. One million retired people were living on incomes below this threshold, but owned more than £100,000 of equivalised housing wealth. This amounts to 10.2 per cent of the overall retired population. They each owned on average £181,000 of housing wealth, £182 billion in total.

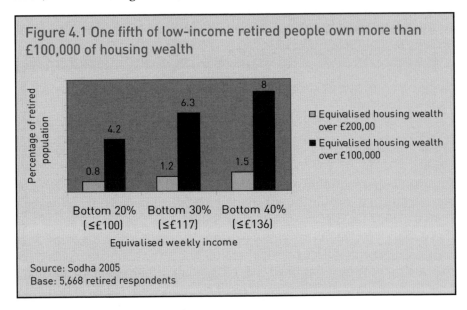

Figure 4.1 One fifth of low-income retired people own more than £100,000 of housing wealth

Source: Sodha 2005
Base: 5,668 retired respondents

The number of asset-rich, income-poor pensioners is likely to rise

In the generation approaching retirement, many of those who will be the poorest pensioners have some access to housing wealth. Almost a quarter of the bottom quintile of the pension wealth distribution of those aged over 50 and yet to retire own more than £100,000 of gross housing wealth each, as shown in Figure 4.2. This figure is higher than for the bottom quintile of the pensioner income distribution. If we assume that they will have paid off their mortgage by the time they reach retirement, they will own £100,000 of net housing wealth at retirement. This figure represents an approximation, as some may not have paid off their mortgage on retirement, but there will also have been capital gains to this housing wealth.

This trend operates against a background of future increases in the level of homeownership among the retired population. Figure 4.3 shows how homeownership levels have changed over time. Those who were 65-74 in 2004 had a homeownership rate of 76 per cent in 2004, compared to 80 per cent for those 45-64. On the basis of previous years, this younger cohort are likely to remain homeowners as they move into retirement, and actually

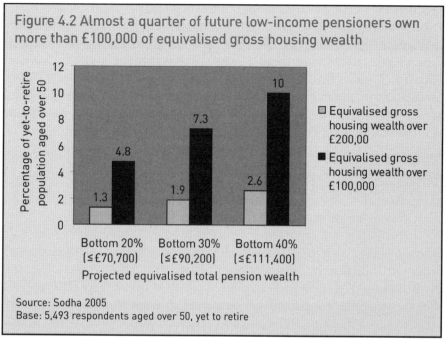

Figure 4.2 Almost a quarter of future low-income pensioners own more than £100,000 of equivalised gross housing wealth

Percentage of yet-to-retire population aged over 50

□ Equivalised gross housing wealth over £200,00

■ Equivalised gross housing wealth over £100,000

Bottom 20% (≤£70,700) — 1.3, 4.8
Bottom 30% (≤£90,200) — 1.9, 7.3
Bottom 40% (≤£111,400) — 2.6, 10

Projected equivalised total pension wealth

Source: Sodha 2005
Base: 5,493 respondents aged over 50, yet to retire

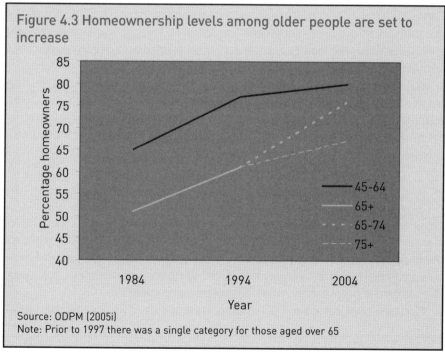

Figure 4.3 Homeownership levels among older people are set to increase

Percentage homeowners

45-64
65+
65-74
75+

1984   1994   2004

Year

Source: ODPM (2005i)
Note: Prior to 1997 there was a single category for those aged over 65

increase the rate of homeownership further. For example, 65 per cent of those aged 45-64 in 1984 were homeowners. Twenty years later, the home-ownership rate among this same group had increased to 76 per cent.

The number of childless couples will increase
The number of pensioners without children is set to grow from 10 to 20 per cent of the pensioner population over the next 20 years (Pensions Commission 2004). Our focus groups showed that the desire to leave an inheritance to children is important in explaining negative attitudes towards equity release, as we outline in Chapter 7 (see also Rowlingson and McKay 2005). This trend might lead to increasing numbers of pensioners who are willing to release housing wealth.

Releasing housing wealth is predicted to become more common

The combination of these demographic factors has led to industry predictions that releasing housing wealth will continue to become more common.

The value of new mortgages reported by the 18 members of the Safe Home Income Plan (SHIP) increased from £6.3 million in 1998 to over £1 billion in 2005 (Equity Release Working Party 2005, SHIP 2006a). Industry predicts that this growth will continue. A survey conducted by SHIP showed that their members expected new business to grow from £1.1 billion in 2005 to £1.4 billion in 2006, and £2 billion in 2008 (SHIP 2006c). In the longer term, a report by the Actuarial Profession (Equity Release Working Party 2005) also had optimistic growth forecasts, based on projections of the number of older homeowners, the reported willingness of different age groups to purchase equity release 'at some point', and average loan sizes and lengths.

These projections are approximate, and we might question the reliability of survey data about people's attitudes to financial decisions in 20 or more years' time. However, as we note above, the political and social drivers of the markets for releasing housing wealth should lead us to expect an increased use of equity release in the future.

Current policy debates increase the importance of housing wealth

The need to examine the release of housing wealth is also driven by policy debates. Housing wealth could contribute to funding gaps around pensions, care, or housing upkeep, all subject to ongoing debate. We need to be clear about which of these gaps housing wealth could fill.

First, the pension system is being re-examined by the Government in the light of the findings and recommendations of the Pensions Commission (2005). Could removing barriers to equity release be a cost-effective way to reduce pensioner poverty? The first report of the Commission suggested that housing cannot provide an escape from the 'unavoidable choices' of allowing pensioners to get poorer relative to the rest of society, raising

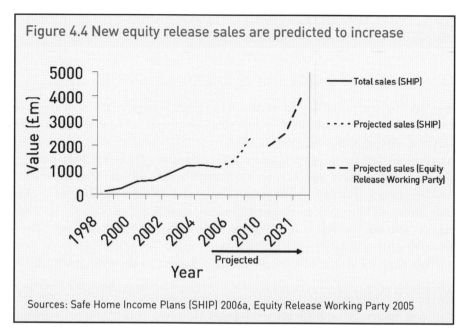

Figure 4.4 New equity release sales are predicted to increase

Value (£m)

5000
4000
3000
2000
1000
0

Total sales (SHIP)

Projected sales (SHIP)

Projected sales (Equity Release Working Party)

1998 2000 2002 2004 2006 2010 2031

Projected

Year

Sources: Safe Home Income Plans (SHIP) 2006a, Equity Release Working Party 2005

average retirement ages, saving more, or paying more in tax/National Insurance for pensions (Pensions Commission 2004). But there may still be scope for improving the use of housing wealth for certain groups.

Similarly, it has been suggested that housing wealth could help pay for long-term personal care in England (Johnstone 2005). But we would challenge this particular use because of its unfair implications. Previous ippr work has recommended that, as a matter of social justice, personal care needs, like nursing care, should be provided free by the state on the basis of need, as is already the case in Scotland (Brooks *et al* 2002). Healthcare needs caused by the diseases of old age should be treated in a consistent way to those caused by acute illnesses. Such a system would not be unaffordable: modelling suggests that the cost would be 0.2 to 0.45 per cent of GDP in 2050 (Brooks *et al* 2002).

The Wanless Social Care Review also recognised that the potential of housing wealth as a source of funding for social care is limited. It concluded that 'out of pockets' payments, for example from the proceeds of equity release, are much more feasible in a 'top-up' model in which the state pays for a minimum level of care, then matches individual contributions up to a benchmark level, than in a system in which some individuals are required to cover the whole cost (Wanless 2006).

Additionally, housing upkeep, supported in the social rented sector by the Decent Homes initiative, is no longer the subject of grants for homeowners. Could the wealth locked up in their homes provide an alternate resource?

Finally, freeing up housing wealth by trading down could contribute to the housing supply. As policies develop in the light of the Barker Review

(2003, 2004), large and expensive houses might be freed up by encouraging pensioners to move into smaller homes.

There are significant barriers to accessing this wealth

It would be tempting to extrapolate from the above analysis that there is £182 billion of housing wealth available for pensioners living below Age Concern's Modest but Adequate standard to tap into. However, we need to be cautious before doing so. There are a number of barriers that exist to accessing this wealth, which we consider further in the next four chapters.

First, housing wealth is inherently expensive to release. Chapter 5 outlines the costs involved in releasing housing wealth. Selling up and renting, equity release products and trading down all bring significant costs, whether upfront or delayed.

This expense is one of the contributing factors to the principled objections older people have to releasing wealth from the home, considered in Chapter 6. These negative attitudes are deep-seated rather than superficial, and will therefore be difficult to change. However, future increases in the number of childless pensioners (Pensions Commission 2004) and different attitudes among the middle-aged generation (Rowlingson and McKay 2005) suggest that pensioner attitudes may become more positive in the future.

Third, the current benefit system acts as a disincentive to those pensioners on means-tested benefits to make use of their own wealth. As detailed in Chapter 7, many pensioners on means-tested benefits would suffer a loss to their benefit income should they release wealth from their homes. The entitlement rules for means-tested benefits are also so complex that it is almost impossible for older people to calculate the effect on their entitlement of increasing their income or capital.

Given this, and the complexity and cost of equity release products, it is crucial that good quality, affordable financial advice is available for asset-rich, income-poor pensioners wanting to release wealth from their home. Chapter 8 outlines how such financial advice has limited quality and availability. This increases the risk of another mis-selling scandal, and means that equity release and trading down may be under-explored options for older people on low incomes.

Chapter 9 looks at the problems specific to trading down, most importantly, the inadequate supply of suitable houses to trade down into.

Conclusions

Housing wealth in retirement is likely to become more important. It is a resource that could be drawn upon for a regular income or property upkeep. Around a fifth of pensioners living in poverty own more than £100,000 of housing wealth, and social trends suggest that this number will increase in the near future. But there are a number of factors that limit the use of housing wealth. We consider the role for government in light of these in the next five chapters.

5. Understanding the markets: pricing and provision

This chapter examines the markets for releasing housing wealth. It finds:

- It is inherently expensive to release housing wealth – either through equity release or trading down.
- Trading down involves meeting the upfront costs of moving, which some have estimated to be £15,000-£20,000 in London and the South East (Jones 2004).
- Equity release products are expensive, because loans are taken out against a home that are not paid back until death, which means that interest rolls up over time. A £20,000 loan taken out today at six per cent annual interest will have accumulated to £64,900 in 30 years' time in today's prices, assuming annual inflation of two per cent.
- However, there is no evidence that equity release products represent substantially worse value for money than conventional mortgages. Lifetime mortgage interest rates are only slightly higher than for conventional mortgages. We might expect this to be the case because of the higher risks taken on by providers.
- The market for lower-value loans is less restricted now than it has been in the past. At least two commercial lenders offer loans as small as £3,000-£5,000. Those in ex-Right to Buy properties, especially flats, have a lower choice of provider, but are still able to purchase a product.

Thus, the case for government subsidy or provision of equity release products is weak. Even if this were the most cost-effective way of improving pensioner poverty, it would distort individual saving decisions in the long term.

How does the market for equity release products work? In this chapter we outline the main features of these markets. Only some wealth can be released from the home, and releasing it is expensive. We also discuss whether there is a role for government on the supply side.

Different ways of releasing wealth

There are many options for an older person who wants to release wealth from a home, outlined in Box 5.1. But, even with optimistic assumptions about market efficiency, none of these methods can release all of the wealth in a home. Different methods may be suitable for pensioners of different ages.

If a homeowner sells and rents, some of the liquefied wealth must be set aside to pay for rent. The longer they expect to live, the more wealth they will need for rent. Selling and renting is therefore more suitable for older pensioners, but would require taking on a significant longevity and house price risk. If rents increase substantially after they have sold their house, or they live much longer than expected, they may find that they have much less wealth left than they anticipated.

Similarly, equity release products may be more suitable for older pensioners. The amount that can be released depends on age, with younger pensioners able to borrow less of their property value, reflecting the fact that the debt is likely to have longer to accumulate. Lump sum lifetime mortgages typically offer 15-20 per cent of the value of a property to someone aged 65, rising to 30 per cent to someone aged 75, and a maximum of 50 per cent for those aged 90 (Curry 2004). The sum that a homeowner will receive in a home reversion in exchange for their property will also increase with age.

Conversely, in trading down, the amount released will depend on the upfront costs of moving, and the availability and suitability of lower-value properties. Trading down is likely to be easier for younger pensioners, as stressed by participants in our seminars. As people become older, they may need more help with the legal and logistical processes of moving, and it could be harder to adjust to a new home. Impaired mobility may also be a problem.

Box 5.1: Ways of releasing housing wealth

Selling and renting
Homeowners can move into rented accommodation, and use the proceeds from the sale of their property to finance the rent. The individual then bears the risk of increases in rent, or living longer than expected

Trading down
Homeowners can sell their current home, and move into a less expensive property. The homeowner will face upfront costs associated with moving (legal fees, surveyor fees, the costs of the physical move, and, in some cases, stamp duty), so the amount of equity released will be substantially less than the difference in values of the two properties.

Lifetime mortgages
A lifetime mortgage allows homeowners to take a loan out against their home that is not paid back until the sale of the property. The money can be taken as a lump sum or as a regular monthly payment. More recent products

cont. next page

also offer a drawdown facility, whereby the loan can be extended in smaller increments, such as £5,000, for a low fixed cost. The interest normally rolls up until the death of the owners, although it is also possible to take out a loan with interest-only repayments. The amount that can be borrowed depends on age, with older homeowners able to borrow more. Most lifetime mortgages have a 'no-negative-equity' guarantee, so the seller or estate will never owe more than the house is worth.

Home reversion
A proportion of the home is sold to a home reversion company for less than its market value. The money can be taken as an annuity or a lump sum. In return, the homeowner can continue to live in the home rent-free. Younger homeowners receive less, because they are likely to continue living in their homes for longer.

Lifetime mortgages and home reversions are collectively referred to in this paper as equity release products.

In addition, there are some government-supported schemes available on a much smaller scale:

Leasehold Schemes for the Elderly (LSE) allow low-income homeowners over the age of 55 to move into part-owned affordable housing. An individual purchases 70 per cent of the market value of a property, and there is no rent to pay on the remaining 30 per cent. In 2004/05, 144 individuals and 45 couples bought through LSE (Joint Centre for Scottish Housing Research 2005).

Shared Ownership for the Elderly (SOFTE) is similar, but allows the buyer to purchase 25, 50 or 75 per cent of the property. If they buy less than 75 per cent, they must pay rent on the share that they do not own, but not on the final 25 per cent. In 2004/05, 39 individuals and 10 couples bought through SOFTE.

Third-sector schemes also offer equity release. The London Rebuilding Society, for example, offers property maintenance to low-income homeowners in return for an equity stake. This is supported by a local authority and the Treasury's Invest to Save Budget.

Releasing wealth is expensive

It is not uncommon to make very optimistic assumptions about the amount that can be released from a home. In a study of the adequacy of retirement resources in the UK, Banks *et al* (2005) assume that 100 per cent of housing wealth can be realised at retirement for those in receipt of the income guarantee portion of Pension Credit, by selling up, renting and claiming Housing Benefit, and that all other homeowners can realise 50 per cent of housing wealth at retirement through trading down or equity release.

But it is difficult to see how these assumptions could ever be realised. If all homeowner pensioners who could, sold up and claimed Housing Benefit, this would have significant cost implications. Housing Benefit expenditure on pensioners would increase dramatically, and capital limits in the means test would need to be lifted.

Similarly, it is difficult to envisage it ever being commercially viable for equity release providers to lend as much as 50 per cent of a property's value to those in their 60s with a no negative equity guarantee. A roll-up loan at six per cent annual interest would have more than trebled in size in 20 years. Unless an older person owns a very large, expensive home, trading down is also unlikely to release 50 per cent of the property's value unless they move from an expensive to a much cheaper area.

Releasing wealth from the home brings costs regardless of the method used. If a pensioner chooses to release wealth by selling and renting, or trading down, they must finance the physical cost of moving, and legal and estate agent fees. Additionally, those trading down will face surveyor fees, and stamp duty if they are moving to a property that is not below the tax-free threshold. Some estimates of the typical costs of moving in London and the South East have put the figure in the region of £15,000-£20,000 (Jones 2004).

Equity release products are also expensive because pensioners continue to live rent-free in their home. The costs are higher the earlier the product is purchased. For example, a £20,000 lifetime mortgage taken out today at age 60 at six per cent annual interest would accumulate to £64,900 in today's prices by age 90, assuming annual inflation of two per cent. The same loan taken out at age 80 today would accumulate to £29,600 by age 90 in today's prices.

Interest rates for lifetime mortgages are slightly higher than for standard mortgages

The interest rates of lifetime mortgages are often higher than standard mortgages, but there is some overlap.

In a telephone survey of SHIP members[4], we found that the lowest fixed rate was 5.79 per cent and the highest fixed rate was 7.2 per cent. In

---

4. We conducted a telephone survey of all lenders who are members of SHIP, as well as three building societies that are not SHIP members (Chorley and District, Dudley, and Vernon). The phone calls were placed between 31 January 2006 and 6 February 2006. Where possible, we also referred to the lenders' websites.

comparison, the best fixed rate for standard mortgages, as published by www.thisismoney.co.uk (8 February 2006), was 6.2 per cent (overall APR).

For variable rates, the lifetime mortgage range was 5.49 to 7.14, compared to a mean for the best-buy standard variable rate mortgages on www.thisismoney.co.uk of 6.0 per cent. The building society average mortgage rate was 5.15 per cent in December 2005 (the latest data available), and the average building society and bank basic mortgage rate (that is, the standard variable rate) was 6.4 per cent (Council of Mortgage Lenders 2006).

A small difference in interest rate can make a large difference to the total cost. For example, if a lifetime mortgage rate is seven per cent rather than six per cent, this will cost consumers an extra £21,600 on a 30-year mortgage of £20,000 in today's prices, assuming annual inflation of two per cent.

Although lifetime mortgages are expensive because interest accumulates over time, there is nothing to suggest that the interest rates represent worse value than standard mortgage interest rates. Providers of lifetime mortgages take on a number of extra risks, which we might expect to be reflected in slightly higher rates. Most providers (95 per cent by market volume) are members of an industry body, Safe Home Income Plans (SHIP), and offer a 'no negative equity' guarantee as part of their code of practice, so customers will never owe more than the value of their home. In addition, extra risk comes from offering long-term fixed interest rates and from longevity uncertainty, which means that providers cannot be sure when the loan will be repaid.

Moreover, the extent to which the real estate is reduced by equity release depends on the retail and house price inflation. Lifetime mortgages tend to have fixed interest rates, so an increase in inflation will reduce their real cost. If the house value increases by the same rate as the rate of interest on their lifetime mortgage, the amount repayable on death will be equivalent to the original loan taken out as a percentage of property value.

Provision at the low-value end of the market has improved

An equity release product involves significant transaction costs, such as valuation and legal fees. Not surprisingly, this has led to a restricted market for lower-value loans, although this is less the case now than at any time in the past. Figure 5.1 shows the minimum loan sizes, including one as low as £3,000. Of the four with the lowest loan sizes, two are only available through local authorities or home improvement trusts.

Aside from the minimum loan size, availability at the bottom of the market can be restricted for those who acquired their property under the right to buy. Of the 16 lenders that are members of SHIP, three automatically disqualify all ex-local authority properties. Other lenders did not reject

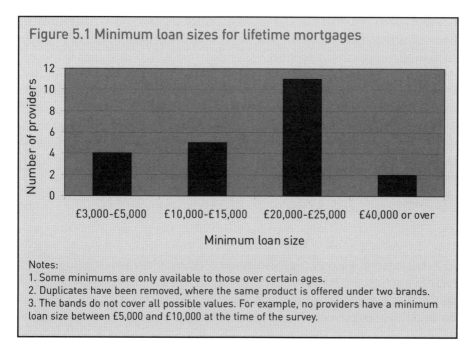

Figure 5.1 Minimum loan sizes for lifetime mortgages

Notes:
1. Some minimums are only available to those over certain ages.
2. Duplicates have been removed, where the same product is offered under two brands.
3. The bands do not cover all possible values. For example, no providers have a minimum loan size between £5,000 and £10,000 at the time of the survey.

these properties outright, but set out a number of conditions. For example, two offer loans against ex-local authority houses, but not flats or maisonettes, and a further one will consider flats, but only if they are located in an area where at least 50 per cent of the flats are privately owned. Over 2.3 million properties in the UK had been purchased via the Right to Buy scheme by 2004 (Wilcox 2005), so many homeowners may face a restricted choice in equity release plans.

Expense is not, in itself, an argument for intervention

Some arguments have been made to us that, because equity release is expensive, and unavailable to those wanting smaller loans, it merits government intervention, perhaps through direct interest subsidy or a transfer of risk to the state. We have not been able to find evidence that the pricing of equity release products does not reflect their extra cost. It is also worth noting that the provision of lower-value loans has improved considerably, although ex-Right to Buy owners still suffer from restricted choice.

A case for subsidy could be made only if spending a certain amount on subsidising releasing housing wealth would do more to alleviate pensioner poverty than spending this money on alleviating poverty directly, for example through pensioner benefits or services. But three factors make this unlikely.

First, the negative attitudes of current pensioners towards equity release products that we describe in the next chapter suggest that many asset-rich, income-poor pensioners would be reluctant to take a loan out against their home, even at very low rates of interest. Subsidising equity release is therefore unlikely to be a more effective way of reducing pensioner poverty than spending on benefits or services.

Second, the distributional impact could be damaging, with asset-rich, income-poor pensioners helped over the poverty threshold, leaving asset-*poor*, income-poor pensioners behind.

Third, a subsidy would distort the retirement saving decisions of those not yet in retirement, diverting saving from pensions to houses. This would go against the current grain of government policy to encourage pension savings as an efficient way of saving for retirement.

Conclusions

This chapter has outlined the different ways of releasing housing wealth, and their associated costs and availability. Those who own housing wealth require a stream of 'housing services' even in retirement, so the amount of wealth that is available for use is substantially below the market value of the home. Older people either need to move to a new property, or, if they wish to continue living in their homes, take a loan out against it to be repaid when the home is sold.

However, that does not mean that housing wealth could not be better used, and, to explore that issue further, we undertook focus groups and in-depth interviews with asset-rich, income-poor pensioners. These are the subject of the following chapter.

6. Attitudes to releasing housing wealth[5]

> This chapter examines attitudes towards releasing housing wealth, based on focus groups and paired interviews carried out for this project. It finds that:
>
> - In general, asset-rich, income-poor pensioners hold similar views to other pensioners, with deep-seated, principled objections to equity release.
>
> - Their attitudes were shaped by five factors: the desire to leave a bequest, the symbolic importance of homeownership, distrust of providers, fear of loss of control and attitudes to debt.
>
> - They were more positive about trading down. Although they raised concerns about upfront costs, emotional upheaval and the impact on social networks and lifestyle, the desire to leave an inheritance was not considered.
>
> - This evidence on attitudes further weakens the case for government subsidy of equity release.
>
> The deep distrust of providers that was expressed suggests that there may be a role for government in extending the regulatory framework to require providers to give a statutory 'no negative equity' guarantee.

The attitudes of asset-rich, income-poor pensioners towards their housing wealth gives an indication of what government action might prove effective, and how important it would be seen to be. Previous research, summarised below, has shown that pensioners are very sceptical of equity release products. We might expect, however, that the attitudes of asset-rich, income-poor pensioners differ from the rest of the pensioner population because of their financial predicament. Our work suggests that this is not the case. Asset-rich, income-poor pensioners do not appear to be more favourably inclined to the idea of equity release.

Previous research

The methodologies used in previous studies on attitudes towards equity release products and trading down is summarised in Table 6.1. This qualitative and survey research has shown that, although homeowners tend to be positive about the general principle of using wealth in their home during their retirement, they are less favourably disposed to specific

---

5   Chapter written with James Morris

methods of doing so, such as equity release and trading down (Rowlingson and McKay 2005, Smith 2004b).

Negative attitudes were shaped by:

- The desire to leave their home as a bequest to their children (Gay 2004, Rowlingson and McKay 2005, Smith 2004b, Sproule *et al* 2004).
- Distrust of the providers (Gay 2004, Rowlingson and McKay 2005).
- Perceived riskiness of the schemes (Gay 2004, Rowlingson and McKay 2005).
- Perceived bad value for money (Gay 2004, Rowlingson and McKay 2005).

Table 6.1 Previous research on attitudes to releasing wealth from the home

Study	Methodology
Rowlingson and McKay (2005)	● National survey of 2,000 respondents, partly selected randomly and partly by quota ● Four focus groups with 26 participants in total, with 12 aged 65+
Gay (2004)	● Four focus groups and 12 in-depth interviews with mostly homeowners aged 55-70 in social classes C2 and D ● Representative survey of 1,000 55-70 year old homeowners
Smith (2004a)	● Face-to-face survey with 2,268 respondents, including tenants and homeowners
Sproule, Roy and Rose (2004)	● Survey of 639 parents and 600 adult children

---

Homeowners tended to be more positive about trading down than other methods of releasing housing wealth. However, there were concerns about the feasibility of releasing wealth by trading down from properties that are already fairly low-value, and about the lifestyle impact of trading down to a cheaper property or area (Gay 2004, Rowlingson and McKay 2005, Smith 2004b). Older homeowners in social classes C2 and D stressed that they wanted to maintain spare rooms for visiting friends and family (Gay 2004).

The older homeowners were, the less likely they were to consider releasing wealth from the home (Smith 2004b). This could be explained by different generational attitudes towards debt, or by attitudes changing as people feel that leaving a bequest is becoming more imminent.

The lower the social class and income group of a homeowner, the less likely they were to consider releasing housing wealth from the home (Gay 2004, Rowlingson and McKay 2005, Smith 2004b). This might be explained by the fact that homeowners from higher social classes are likely to own more valuable properties, so can release some wealth from their home while still leaving a substantial bequest.

Our focus groups

As part of this project, we carried out focus groups and paired interviews with asset-rich, income-poor pensioners. They revealed that these pensioners had deep-seated, principled objections to equity release that it would be difficult for government to change, should it decide to promote the use of housing wealth.

We spoke to 30 asset-rich, income-poor pensioners. All owned a house worth between £100,000 and £300,000. Half were 'low income', with incomes roughly below the lowest quintile level, calculated as below £105 per week (single) or £160 per week (couple). Half fell into the 'mid income' category, with income above the 'low income' group, but under the level equivalent to the 'modest but adequate' benchmark used by Age Concern (2002), calculated as incomes below £150 per week (single) or £250 per week (couple).

We discussed with participants whether they felt their retirement income was adequate, and found that dissatisfaction with current incomes was related to age more than actual income level. Older pensioners regarded their income as just enough with which to get by, but the younger age group were less satisfied. This is consistent with other research, which has shown that, although older pensioners have fewer material resources on average than younger pensioners, they tend to have higher levels of financial satisfaction (Burholt and Windle 2006).

We also discussed whether they would consider releasing wealth from the home through a variety of methods, including renting out a room, selling and renting, trading down and equity release schemes. Finally, we explored views on different forms of government intervention.

We present our methodology in more detail in the annex to this chapter (p64). Our work should be regarded as indicative rather than conclusive because of the small numbers involved. But it suggests that the attitudes of asset-rich, income-poor pensioners do not differ from the rest of the pensioner population, as we might perhaps expect.

Attitudes towards equity release products

All participants were familiar with the general principle of equity release schemes, although some were more knowledgeable than others on the details. A few had seen equity release products advertised on television, and had read about them in newspapers. There was a greater awareness of home reversion schemes than lifetime mortgages.

In general, all participants bar one were very negative. There was deeply held opposition to the principle of either selling part of the home or accumulating debt against it. Most people felt that they had spent their working lives saving towards their home, and that it was not a resource they were prepared to tap into in their old age.

> You've saved and gone without, you don't want to give a bit of your house up. (low income, 65-74)

> It's a terrible imposition when you've worked for years to build it up – an imposition on your generosity. (low income, 75+)

> I feel fidgety about the whole thing, it's taken years and years of hard graft to get where I am and no one can take that away. (low income, 75+)

> I'd sell up a lot – like my car – before I gave up my house. (mid income, 65-74)

Participants were asked whether there were any changes in circumstance that might lead them to consider taking out an equity release scheme. The overall consensus was that either they or their family would have to be 'desperate' for them to consider these schemes.

> I would think about it, but I'd need to be desperate. (low income, 75)

> If you're on the breadline, you'd consider anything. (mid income, 65-74)

> These are last resort schemes. (mid income, 65-74)

Participants' attitudes to equity release products seemed to be shaped by five critical factors: the desire to leave a bequest, distrust of providers, the symbolic importance of ownership, attitudes towards debt and the desire to remain in control of their own financial affairs.

The desire to leave a bequest is critical

The desire to leave a bequest for children and grandchildren seemed to be the most important factor in shaping opinions on equity release. All the homeowners we spoke to had children, and all but one felt that the implications of equity release for the inheritance they would be able to leave their children and grandchildren made it extremely unattractive.

> It's something you've saved into, and you want it all to go to your kids. (low income, 65-74)

> It's robbing the heirs. (mid income, 75+)

> The home is all we have to pass on. (mid income, 75+)

> The children come first. (low income, 75+)

There was consensus that equity release would be an attractive option if you did not have children.

If you had no family ties, it'd be great. (mid income, 65-74)

If I were single, I'd have a whale of a time. (low income, 65-74)

The only participant who said she would consider equity release said this was because her children had told her that she should feel free to release equity from her home rather than leave it as a bequest for them.

There is a pervasive distrust of equity release providers

There was a deep-seated cynicism about these schemes and whether they presented value for money, especially when participants were presented with examples of what a lifetime mortgage or home reversion might cost. This was particularly true in the group aged 65-74. Participants believed that companies would make a huge amount of profit from these schemes. They felt that the financial services industry was deliberately targeting older people to make an easy profit, and were strongly opposed to the principle of selling the home below market value or rolling up debt over the years.

They rely on older people being stupid. (low income, 65-74)

I'm horrified. It's sheer robbery. (mid income, 65-74)

They're just out to get your money. (mid income, 65-74)

There's only one winner: the company. It's got to be a con. (mid income, 65-74)

It's a conspiracy to get to our wealth. (mid income, 65-74)

Ownership has deep symbolic importance

Participants were very negative about selling their home and renting as a way of releasing housing wealth. For many, it was tied to issues about status: they felt that they had saved during their working lives in order to become homeowners and that to sell up and rent would be a step backwards.

It'd be going backwards. (low income, 65-74)

I've worked all my life – I'm not going to give my house up. (mid income, 65-74)

Attitudes to equity release products were tainted by the same symbolic loss of ownership. One couple who had considered a home reversion product said they immediately changed their mind when they realised it would mean physically handing over the deeds to the house.

When you pay your mortgage you're free of it – this is going back, a backwards step. (mid income, 65-74)

Equity release was equated with a loss of control

Participants felt that equity release schemes would reduce their flexibility should they need to move later on, and were worried about providers going bankrupt and consequently threatening the security of the home.

You'd lack control over your own destiny. (mid income, 65-74)

At least with downsizing, there's no one else pulling the strings. (mid income, 65-74)

They also strongly disliked the uncertainly about the amount that would need to be repaid on death in a conventional lifetime mortgage.

My first thought looking at the numbers is that you wouldn't want to live until you were ninety! (low income, 75+)

Attitudes to debt were important in the older age group

Attitudes to debt were important in influencing opinions of equity release in the older age category, 75+. Most of this group were opposed to the idea of taking on debt. One mid-income participant thought that turning to equity release would be a reflection that someone had not managed their finances as well as they could have done.

What we can't afford, we don't have. (mid income, 75+)

I couldn't do that – money doesn't mean anything anymore. (low income, 75+)

Trading down

Participants were generally more positive about trading down as a way to release wealth from the home because it involves retaining full ownership, but a different set of concerns emerged.

The younger, low-income group was the most positive about the idea. About a third of those from this group, in fact, had already released wealth from their home by moving to a smaller property since their children had left home. Some mentioned that they would have liked to, but did not have the upfront capital they would have needed to do so.

Interestingly, no participant mentioned a desire to leave an inheritance – so important in shaping attitudes towards equity release – as something that would make them reluctant to trade down. This is despite the fact that trading down also reduces the total size of bequests that someone can leave.

On concerns about trading down, all age groups and income levels stressed the importance of existing social networks. All participants were reluctant to move area, stressing the value they placed on living close to family and friends. There was a great deal of emphasis on the importance of good neighbours: moving was thought to be a substantial risk as new neighbours could be less friendly or helpful.

For the older group, their emotional attachment to the home was the most important objection. They felt that moving would be a traumatic and difficult experience, and that they had accumulated too much to be able to move to a smaller house. Any move would be because of deteriorating health, rather than financial reasons – for example, to an adapted property, or to sheltered housing.

> Our home has been a shelter over the years – we wouldn't want to leave it now. (low income, 75+)

> We don't like change. (low income, 75+)

> The thought of moving is very traumatic, I love my house. (low income, 75+)

Like the older group, the mid-income group was less positive about trading down, in this case because they were concerned with the practical and lifestyle implications of trading down. Some said the costs of moving were too high, and thought that the gap between the price of the two properties involved would have to be fairly substantial in order to cover those costs and make the move worthwhile. Others mentioned that moving to a smaller property might mean investing in furniture to fit new specifications.

For others, implications for lifestyle were very important. They felt that moving to a smaller property could result in them having less privacy if they moved from a detached or semi-detached home to a terraced house or a flat, and less security if they moved to a cheaper area.

> I wouldn't want to downgrade socially. (mid income, 75+)

> Downsizing would mean downsizing in lifestyle too – you can't find a two bed detached house, and that's what we're used to. (mid income, 65-74)

We discuss the implications of more positive attitudes towards trading down in Chapter 9.

Views about possible government interventions

Participants were provided with a list of possible government interventions to help people release wealth from their homes:

- Helping older people find a suitable home to move into.
- Financial and practical help with moving.
- Lower stamp duty for older people trading down.
- Free advice about what kinds of equity release products are available.
- Exempting from the benefit means test money released from the home, either from equity release products or trading down.

They were asked which they thought would be helpful, and which they thought should be prioritised.

It was difficult to engage participants in a detailed discussion about these issues because they were so negative about the principle of equity release. Most thought all of the above would be helpful to some extent, but that they would not make a big difference to whether or not they decided to release equity.

Some participants thought free advice about equity release might make them feel more positively inclined towards it, but others felt that they might not trust government to deliver impartial advice on financial issues.

Participants were also asked whether they would have more confidence in the products on offer if they were endorsed by organisations such as Help the Aged or Age Concern. A couple of participants said they could not envisage these organisations ever endorsing an equity release product. None were aware that there are already lifetime mortgages branded by these organisations on the market, and all were surprised to hear this.

With regard to a possible benefit means test exemption for liquidised housing wealth, many participants found it difficult to understand the issues involved. Those that expressed a preference thought that it would make equity release more attractive for those entitled to benefits. But this question led most participants to discuss the complexities of the benefits system and the fact that many of them did not understand why they were or were not entitled to benefits.

When pressed on prioritisation, most participants focused on the interventions on the list concerned with trading down rather than equity release.

Help finding a home and moving was said to be of only limited use if there was a lack of affordable or suitable housing for them to move to. Some suggested that there should be more affordable accommodation for older people available for rent or purchase.

If they built really nice flats, that might be an incentive to move. (mid income, 65-74)

It's not just finding a home, it's finding an affordable home. (mid income, 65-74)

Stamp duty was unpopular. Most participants felt that the level of stamp duty was too high in general, and that the threshold should be higher, or the tax should be abolished altogether on principle.

Conclusions

The small sample size means that these findings are indicative rather than conclusive. But our work with asset-rich, income-poor pensioners broadly supports the findings of previous research into the attitudes of older people more generally. Participants' views on using housing wealth were driven by the importance of ownership, attitudes to inheritance, distrust of providers, lifestyle factors, and the desire to remain in control of their own financial affairs.

Participants were more positive about trading down than equity release. Why did they find it acceptable to reduce the amount available for bequests by releasing wealth from the home by trading down, but not equity release? This might partly be because the 'cost' of releasing the wealth is shared between the recipients (who inherit a smaller house) and the donors (who live in a smaller house), rather than falling wholly on recipients.

Other likely explanations include debt aversion and dislike of the uncertainty involved in a roll-up lifetime mortgage: the total amount owed depends on when they die. If this is the case, lifetime mortgages that require repayment of interest during the life of the borrower, and therefore involve a fixed repayment on death to the value of the original loan, might be more popular.

Negative attitudes towards equity release might change in the future as the baby boomer generation reaches retirement. Younger homeowners in their 40s and 50s appear to be more favourable to the idea of using assets in their own lifetimes rather than bequeathing them.

In a recent survey of 2,000 people, 46 per cent of those aged 45-54 said they would be likely to release wealth from their home in the future, but only 37 per cent aged 65-80 said they would do so (Smith 2004b). Similarly, 66 per cent of those aged 45-54 said they would consider trading down, compared to 48 per cent of those aged 65-80, and 13 per cent of those aged 45-54 said they would consider equity release, but only two per cent aged 65-80 said they would. Only 40 per cent of homeowners aged 45-60 said they wanted to leave their whole house as a bequest for their children, compared to 64 per cent of those aged 65-80.

We cannot be sure whether these are life stage or cohort effects. People's statements about what financial decisions they intend to make in 20 years' time are unlikely to prove to be accurate, and views may change as they come closer to the end of their lives. But there is certainly a possibility that equity release might be more popular among younger generations when they reach retirement.

Furthermore, the Government's efforts to introduce shared ownership for younger households may popularise home reversion schemes for older people, also based on this concept. When subtler gradations of tenure become more common it may be that buying a home reversion product will not involve such a large symbolic step.

High current levels of hostility towards equity release products further reinforce the view that government should be cautious in how it involves itself with equity release. Participants in these focus groups did not respond positively to government support, and subsidies are unlikely to be effective in encouraging older people to release equity unless there is a change in the deep-seated negative attitudes towards the products held by many pensioners.

But this does not mean that government should do nothing on the supply side. Our focus groups, as well as previous research (Gay 2004, Rowlingson and McKay 2005), showed that there is a high level of distrust of equity release. In many ways, older homeowners are right to be wary. Equity release is expensive, and unscrupulous salesmen of different products have been known to target old and vulnerable people. While there are some household names (including Northern Rock, Norwich Union, Portman, Prudential, Scottish Widows and Standard Life), there is also a large number of lesser-known brands and dedicated providers. This may contribute to a general sense of mistrust.

An important step in combating this distrust has already been taken by the Government, with the introduction of FSA regulation of lifetime mortgages in November 2004, and an announcement in May 2005 that regulation of home reversion schemes will soon follow. However, this regulation could go a step further, in particular looking at strengthening of the guarantee that consumers will never owe more than the value of their house on death.

While 95 per cent of the market is covered by the Safe Home Income Plans (SHIP) 'no-negative-equity guarantee' (see Box 6.1), this level of guarantee is weak because it is entirely voluntary. If, for example, the company withdraws from SHIP, perhaps because it ceases to offer equity release or because it is taken over, there would be no recourse to appeal. If regulation of lifetime mortgages was extended to include a statutory 'no negative equity' guarantee, this could help to improve provider reputation. The Government should:

- consider extending its regulation of lifetime mortgages to requiring providers to give a no-negative-equity guarantee.

Box 6.1: SHIP Code of Practice

- The members of SHIP agree to provide fair, simple and complete presentation of their plans. The benefits, obligations, variables and limitations must be clearly set out in their literature, including all costs which the applicant has to bear in setting up the scheme, the position on moving, the tax situation and the effect of changes in house values.
- The client's legal work will always be performed by the solicitor of his or her choice. In all cases, prior to the completion of the plan the solicitor will be provided with full details of the benefits the client will receive. The solicitor will be required to sign a certificate to the effect that the scheme has been explained to the client.
- The SHIP certificate will clearly state the main cost to the householder's assets and estate, for example, how the loan amount will change or whether part or all of the property is being sold.
- All SHIP plans carry a 'no negative equity' guarantee, so customers will never owe more than the value of their home.

Source: www.ship-ltd.org/code/index.shtml (accessed 07.02.06)

Previous research supports our finding that trading down was more positively regarded by older people (Gay 2004, Rowlingson and McKay 2005, Smith 2004b). However, older people were concerned about a lack of affordable housing to trade down into. This suggests that trading down might be an easier route through which to encourage older people to draw on their housing wealth in retirement. We consider the role for government in this area in Chapter 9.

Annex to Chapter 6: Qualitative research methodology

Qualitative research is the best methodology for exploring attitudes and beliefs that underpin the way people think, and moves beyond the 'surface level' responses that tend to be elicited by quantitative surveys. It offers an opportunity to map patterns of thinking and highlight areas of consensus and difference (Edwards *et al* 2003).

Research was structured in order to seek the views of two different age groups: those aged 65 to 74, and those aged 75+. We recruited 30 'housing-rich, income poor', respondents for this study, who were aged 65+. All but two were retired homeowners who jointly or solely owned homes worth between £100,000 and £300,000. The two respondents that did not fit these criteria are discounted in the rest of this study.

Recruitment was carried out by a professional company. Two income categories were recruited:

- A lower-income category with incomes of less than £105 per week (single) and £160 per week (couple). These incomes represent the income associated with the 21st percentile in the 2002/03 English Longitudinal Study of Ageing, uprated to 2004 prices, equivalised according to the OECD equivalence scale. In 2002/03, 21 per cent of pensioners lived in poverty.[6]
- A mid-income category with incomes of less than £170 per week (single) and £250 per week (couple). These incomes represent the Age Concern 'Modest but Adequate' benchmark, uprated to 2004 prices.[7]

Participants were in two age categories:

- Aged 65-74.
- Aged 75+.

---

6. Department for Work and Pensions, Households Below Average Income 1995/95-2002/03 (London: The Stationery Office, 2003).
7. (1) Level 1 (21st percentile): £105 for a single pensioner, uprated from £102 in FRS 2002/03 (£102 x 1.047 (earnings increase for 2004) = 106.79, so 105 rounded to nearest 5).
For a couple, £160 (106.79x1.5 (OECD equivalence scale used in ELSA) gives £160 to nearest 5).
(2) Level 2: Age Concern MBA from 2002 uprated to 2004 prices.
Single pensioner, £170 (£158.50 x 1.028 (earnings increase 2003) x 1.047 = £170.59, so £170 to nearest 5).
Couple, £250-£255 (either equivalising the above using OECD scale: £170.549 x 1.5 = £255.89; or Age Concern couple level 2002: 233 x 1.028 x 1.047 = £250.78).

Discussion took place in three focus groups (each with eight respondents) and three paired depth interviews:

- Focus group 1: low income, aged 65-74.
- Focus group 2: mid income, aged 65-74.
- Focus group 3: mixed income (four low and four mid income), aged 65-74.
- In-depth interview 1: low income, aged 75+, single households.
- In-depth interview 2: mid income, aged 75+, members of two joint households.
- In-depth interview 3: mid income, aged 75+, joint household.

All of these took place in Crawley in West Sussex.

All respondents had children and grandchildren. Most had lived in Crawley or the surrounding area for a considerable length of time, around 40 years or more. This was especially true in the lower-income group, perhaps reflecting the fact that house prices in the South East have risen substantially in the past 20 years and that all our respondents were homeowners. All respondents were retired, although a couple in the mid-income group worked occasionally providing services such as gardening and hairdressing.

7. Equity release and the benefits system

This chapter looks at the disincentives that the benefits system creates to releasing housing wealth. It finds that:
- For many pensioners on means-tested benefits, releasing wealth from their home would not be financially worthwhile, as it would reduce their benefit income. In total, 8.2 per cent of pensioners, almost one million individuals, own more than £100,000 of equivalised housing wealth, but are on means-tested benefits. They own on average £183,000 of housing wealth each, and £169 billion in total.
- The complexity of the benefit system makes it difficult for pensioners to predict the effects of releasing wealth on their entitlement.

These disincentives further strengthen the already substantial case for eliminating means-tested Pension Credit and replacing it with a non means-tested British State Pension at the level of guarantee credit, as recommended in previous ippr work (Brooks *et al* 2002).

This is a long-term challenge. In the interim, the Government should:
- make available an online benefits calculator for pensioners that would enable them to determine the effect of increasing their income or capital on their benefit eligibility.

For many pensioners in receipt of means-tested benefits, releasing wealth from the home simply does not pay. Released housing wealth, whether taken as an income or a lump sum, counts against the means test and, in many cases, will reduce benefit entitlement. On top of this, the benefit system is so complex that it is difficult for individuals to predict whether or not releasing wealth will reduce their own entitlement. This is not an insignificant problem. Data from the 2002-03 English Longitudinal Study of Ageing suggests that 4.7 million pensioner homeowners are affected. Of these, 900,000 own more than £100,000 of equivalised housing wealth.

Demand at the lower end of the market is constrained by benefit policies

For homeowners wanting to take out smaller loans, the availability and attractiveness of equity release is already constrained because fixed costs, such as legal advice and surveys, represent a larger proportion of the loan.

If these homeowners are in receipt of means-tested benefits, there is an extra disincentive, and the decision becomes even more complex.

Means tests act as a disincentive to those on low incomes

Many of today's benefits for pensioners, including Pension Credit, Council Tax Benefit and Housing Benefit, are means tested. The amount of benefit a pensioner will receive depends on their income and the amount of capital they have. However, a homeowner's primary residence is exempt from the means test. This creates the anomaly that, while a pensioner's wealth is locked up in their home, it is not counted in the means test, but it is as soon as it is released. So, for many pensioners, it is not financially worthwhile for them to use the resources in the home to boost their income in retirement. Their decision to release wealth is effectively taxed through a reduction in their benefit income.

Benefit eligibility rules are very complex, which creates additional problems, discussed below. Key benefits are outlined in more detail in Box 7.1. To summarise, a pensioner's benefit entitlement would be reduced by releasing housing wealth under the following circumstances:

1. If a pensioner is in receipt of *Pension Credit* (PC), releasing housing wealth as an income stream, or as a lump sum that takes them above the £6,000 capital threshold, will reduce their benefit entitlement unless:
   - they spend the capital in a way not deemed to be 'notional' within their Assessed Income Period (AIP) of five years
   - they spend the capital on essential home improvements within one year.

   So the disincentive that is created by PC entitlement is much smaller for pensioners releasing a lump sum, and well within their five-year AIP, than for pensioners who want to release wealth from their home in order to provide a steady income stream.
2. If a pensioner is in receipt of *Council Tax Benefit* (CTB), releasing housing wealth as an income stream will reduce entitlement to benefits unless they are still entitled to guarantee credit after releasing the wealth. Releasing housing wealth as a lump sum will reduce benefit entitlement if it takes them above the £6,000 capital threshold, unless they are still entitled to the guarantee credit part of PC after releasing the wealth.
3. If a pensioner is in receipt of *free dental treatment and glasses*, releasing housing wealth as an income or lump sum will end this entitlement if it makes them no longer eligible for the guarantee credit part of PC.

How widespread is this problem? Our analysis of the English Longitudinal Study of Ageing suggests that 4.7 million homeowner pensioners would see their benefit income reduced as a result of releasing wealth from their

Box 7.1: Means-tested pensioner benefits

Homeowner pensioners may be eligible for the following means-tested benefits:

Pension Credit

Pension Credit (PC) is means tested and unrelated to National Insurance contributions, unlike the basic state pension. There are two components of PC, a *guarantee credit* that tops up all those aged 60 or over to a minimum weekly income level of £114.05 (single pensioners) or £174.05 (couples) in 2006-07, and *savings credit* for those aged over 65, which is received by pensioners with a weekly income of less than £152.05 (single) and who have some savings.

For those with incomes above the PC guarantee credit level, but below the savings credit upper threshold, the amount of PC they receive tapers off as their income rises. Savings credit operates alongside guarantee credit to create a 40 per cent withdrawal rate for those on the benefit taper, so for every extra pound of income from other sources, pension credit is reduced by 40 pence. The means test is mainly income-based, but also takes capital into account. Any savings of under £6,000 (£10,000 for pensioners in a nursing home) are ignored. Any capital above this level is assumed to produce a weekly income of £1 for every £500 or part thereof.

Most of those aged over 65 have an 'Assessed Income Period' (AIP), which means they are only subject to a means test every five years, and do not need to report changes in circumstance during this time. An increase in income or capital will therefore only affect PC entitlement when the AIP has come to an end, unless they are deemed to have deliberately deprived themselves of capital in order to get Pension Credit, in which case this capital is known as 'notional capital'.

Council Tax Benefit

Council Tax Benefit (CTB) is related to eligibility for PC. If a pensioner's pre-PC weekly income is below the guarantee component of PC they are automatically entitled to full CTB, regardless of any capital they might own. All those with capital over £16,000 are ineligible for CTB regardless of their income level, unless they are eligible for the guarantee component of PC.

For those not in receipt of the guarantee portion of PC, and with capital less than £16,000, entitlement to CTB is means-tested. Capital over £6,000 is assumed to contribute to weekly income in the same way as in the PC means test. Thus, CTB entitlement falls as income rises. For those not in receipt of guarantee credit, CTB is withdrawn at a rate of 20 per cent, so for every extra pound of income from other sources, CTB is reduced by 20 pence. Homeowners on the CTB and PC taper face an effective marginal tax rate of 52 per cent, made up of 20 per cent for CTB, plus 40 per cent of the remaining 80 per cent for PC.

Health benefits
Those who receive the guarantee portion of PC receive free dental treatment and glasses. Other NHS services are free to all pensioners.

Sources: Council of Mortgage Lenders (2005), Clark (2002), Age Concern (2003), www.thepensionservice.gov.uk/pensioncredit

home, assuming that they are nearing the end of their Assessed Income Period (see the annex to this chapter, p73, for details of methodology). Of these, 900,000 own over £100,000 of equivalised housing wealth – equivalent to 8.2 per cent of all pensioners. They own on average £183,000 of housing wealth each, and £169 billion in total, as shown in Table 7.1.

Table 7.1 Asset-rich pensioners on benefits

	Number (millions)	Percent of all pensioners	Mean housing wealth (£)	Total housing wealth (£ billions)
Homeowner pensioners	7.8	72.8	115,000	897
Homeowner pensioners on PC, who own more than £80,000 of equivalised housing wealth	1.3	12.6	155,000	208
Homeowner pensioners on PC, who own more than £100,000 of equivalised housing wealth	0.9	8.6	183,000	169

Note: See annex for methodology and sources

This problem will become even more widespread as the number of pensioners in receipt of PC increases over time. Estimates from the Institute for Fiscal Studies suggest that, by 2050, up to 73 per cent of pensioners will be eligible for Pension Credit, compared to 52 per cent in 2003 (Brewer and Emmerson 2003). Similarly, the Pensions Commission projects that 74 per cent of pensioners will be entitled to Pension Credit in 2050, if current indexing continues indefinitely (Pensions Commission 2005, figure Ex.2).

Complexity makes it difficult to predict the impact of releasing wealth on benefits

As illustrated by the discussion in Box 7.1, the UK has 'the most complex pension system in the world' (Pensions Commission 2004: 210). For individuals in receipt of benefits, it is almost impossible for them to predict the effect of releasing wealth on their benefit entitlement. In focus groups for this project, no older person that we spoke to had a clear idea of how benefit entitlement works, or of the effect on it of releasing housing wealth.

Complexity also makes it more expensive and difficult for advisers and product providers to give advice on the suitability of equity release products for individuals on benefits. A Financial Services Authority mystery shopping exercise in May 2005 found that 74 per cent of advisers approached failed to ask about benefit eligibility (Financial Services Authority 2005c). This issue is explored in more detail in the following chapter.

The disincentives strengthen other arguments in favour of ending Pension Credit means testing

It is a perverse feature of the current system that pensioners wishing to use their own resources to boost their income in retirement should be penalised by a reduction in their benefits. The principle is the same as for saving for retirement. The current means-tested system acts as a disincentive to individuals to save for retirement (Paxton *et al* 2005). Past work by ippr has recommended that means testing of Pension Credit be abolished in order to correct this anomaly (Brooks *et al* 2002, Paxton *et al* 2005). The effect of the current system on incentives to use housing wealth further strengthens these arguments, which are already substantial.

As the Pensions Commission highlighted, there are four options available with respect to government policy towards pensioners: for pensioners to become poorer relative to the rest of society, for taxes to increase, for people to save more, or for the retirement age to increase.

Previous ippr work has argued that that the right strategy would be to encourage people to save more and work longer. Increasing the incentive to save for retirement would be best achieved by abolishing Pension Credit, uprating the British State Pension to the level of guarantee credit (£114.05 for a single pensioner from April 2006), and indexing it with earnings. This would ensure that all pensioners with full contribution records have an income above 60 per cent of the national median. Such a reform would also be affordable if coupled with the phasing out of the State Second Pension and an increase in the state retirement age to 67 (Brooks *et al* 2002).

The proposals of the Pensions Commission do little to increase simplicity. Most of the existing features of the current system would remain, with two state pensions, potentially with different entitlement rules, a significant role for Pension Credit, and the National Pensions Savings System, an entirely new element.

Therefore, the Government should:

- eliminate means-tested Pension Credit and replace it with a non-means-tested British State Pension at the level of guarantee credit, as recommended in previous ippr work (Brooks *et al* 2002, Paxton *et al* 2005).

We should not be overly optimistic about the impact of such a change on the amounts of housing wealth released by the current generation of pensioners. As we have outlined above, many pensioners who are asset-rich and income-poor have negative attitudes towards equity release. Nor is any claim made that the issue of housing wealth alone is sufficiently important to justify such a large change to the pensions system. But pensioners should not be penalised for drawing on their own wealth in retirement, and this is another argument for moving to a system that is fairer as well as affordable. If pensioners of the future warm to the idea of equity release more than the current cohort, this anomaly is likely to become even more pronounced, especially as increasing numbers of pensioners become eligible for means-tested benefits.

This still leaves the issue of Council Tax Benefit, which is also means-tested. Replacing PC with a non-means-tested British State Pension would significantly reduce the disincentive to release housing wealth, but would not eliminate it altogether. The Lyons Inquiry will be examining Council Tax Benefit, and should consider how it relates to asset-rich, income-poor pensioners as a matter of priority (Lyons Inquiry into Local Government 2005).

Reform to the pensions system is a long-term challenge. In the interim, the Government should:

- make available a free online calculator for pensioners that can work out the effect of increasing their income or capital on benefit entitlement. Similar tools developed by the FSA, the Financial Healthcheck and the Debt Test, have been made available on both the FSA and the BBC websites. Their outreach has been significant; the Healthcheck has been used by almost half a million consumers, and the Debt Test by a quarter of a million (Briault 2006).

This kind of benefit software already exists. Ferret Information Systems, in conjunction with the Council of Mortgage Lenders, has developed software that calculates the effect of releasing housing wealth on benefit entitlement (Council of Mortgage Lenders and Ferret 2004). This software reduces the margin of error in predicting whether buying an equity release product or trading down would reduce benefit entitlement. However, it comes at significant cost and is only available to financial intermediaries. For a single user, the first year annual licence and training fee is £611 including VAT, with each further user charged at £545.[8] Alternatively, financial advisers can purchase the software on a single-use, per-case basis at a price of £53 including VAT.

Government could take advantage of economies of scale by developing its own version of this software, and making it available free-of-charge to all on the internet. It should calculate the impact of increasing amounts of capital or income on benefit entitlement in a way simple and open enough to be used by consumers. As well as helping the client group, this would improve the transparency of the system.

Conclusions

For many pensioners on means-tested benefits, the benefits system is a disincentive to boosting income by releasing wealth from the home. Doing so would result in a fall in benefit income. This anomaly adds to the already-strong case that exists for abolishing the means-tested Pension Credit, and replacing it with a non-means-tested British State Pension, set at the guarantee level of Pension Credit. A renewed drive for simplicity should form a major part of the pensions reform following the White Paper released in May 2006. In the interim, the Government should make available a free online benefits calculator for pensioners, so that they are able to determine the effects of increasing their income or capital on their benefit eligibility.

---

8.   Pricing correct as of 11 April 2006, information from www.ferret.co.uk/data/downloads/
     getfile.aspx?path=guides/notes/&item_id=gui-note-fi tal3 and www.ferret.co.uk/fintal-
     aspx/index.aspx?menu=fintalppc

Annex to Chapter 7: Calculating the number of pensioners who would face a reduction in benefits as a result of releasing wealth from their home

In order to estimate the number of asset-rich, income-poor pensioners who would experience a loss in benefits as a result of releasing housing wealth under the current system, we can use data from the 2002-03 English Longitudinal Study of Ageing (ELSA) (Sodha 2005).

To do so, we have to ignore the effect of the Assessed Income Period, as this information is not included in ELSA. We also assume that all those in receipt of means-tested benefits (Pension Credit (PC), Council Tax Benefit (CTB) and/or health benefits) will face some loss to benefits should they choose to release wealth in today's system. This is justified because most people releasing wealth through equity release or trading down will release more than £6,000, the capital threshold, given the high fixed costs of either method. So, equity release or trading down would place all pensioners in receipt of benefits, on a benefit taper. However, an individual's effective marginal tax rate for the released wealth would depend on their income and wealth levels before they released housing wealth and the combination of benefits they receive.

PC did not exist in 2002/03, but, since its introduction, the savings credit, relevant for calculating the uppermost income threshold beyond which no PC is received, has been uprated each year in line with the Retail Price Index (RPI) or at 2.5 per cent, whichever is higher (Hansard 2004). In 2005/06, the income level beyond which single pensioners receive no PC guarantee or savings credit was £152.05 (Council of Mortgage Lenders 2005). Had PC existed in 2003, the threshold would have therefore been £143 (to the nearest pound).[9]

The major benefits paid on top of Pension Credit for pensioners are Council Tax Benefit and Housing Benefit. As the definition of income in ELSA excludes these two benefits, the percentage of the sample below this threshold will represent a rough estimation of the number of people on the benefits taper (although it will not include those who do not receive any PC but who are in receipt of CTB). This is an estimate rather than a precise figure: included in the ELSA definition of income is actual income from financial wealth, but the PC means test ignores the first £6,000 of financial

---

9   National Statistics (2005c)

wealth and assumes a high flat rate of return above this (10.4 per cent per annum). So, for lower levels of financial wealth, ELSA is likely to underestimate PC entitlement, and for higher levels, it is likely to overestimate it.

According to the Department for Work and Pensions (2004b), there were 10.7 million pensioners living in the UK in 2004, and we use this figure to estimate the total number of asset-rich, income-poor pensioners on benefits.

8. Equity release and personalised advice

The complexity of the benefits system outlined in Chapter 7 makes it particularly important that there is good quality, affordable financial advice for older people interested in releasing wealth from their home. This chapter considers the extent to which this is available. It finds:

- There is inadequate financial advice available for asset-rich, income-poor pensioners. Independent product-specific advice is expensive and of variable quality. Free, generic financial advice is not widely available.

Financial advice can help avoid the risk of equity release mis-selling to a potentially vulnerable group, and can ensure that equity release and trading down are options that are considered by retired homeowners on low incomes. There is therefore a role for government in filling the advice gap:

- Regulation of product-specific advice needs to be improved. The FSA should conduct an annual deterrent mystery shopping exercise.
- Government should establish 'MoneyDoctor', a generic financial advice service for older people. This should offer a combination of telephone and face-to-face advice, and carry strong independent branding.
- This service should be used to facilitate *pro bono* work by independent financial advisers, by providing client-matching, training and insurance – as LawWorks does for the legal profession.
- Government should encourage equity release providers and other financial services firms to support the scheme, as one way of reducing the widespread distrust of these products that is constraining take-up.

For pensioners thinking about releasing wealth from their home, getting financial advice is a necessity rather than a luxury. But it is one that few can afford, and is poorly provided by the market. The Financial Services Authority (FSA) recommends that all individuals taking out an equity release product should seek independent financial advice from an FSA-authorised adviser, and with good reason. They are complex legal contracts, and releasing wealth from the home can have significant implications for the size of an estate and tax liabilities.

Significantly for those on low incomes, releasing housing wealth can affect benefit eligibility in ways that are not easy to predict. So financial advice is important in making sure that older people do not buy inappropriate financial products. This is particularly the case for asset-rich, income-poor pensioners on benefits. It can also help older people living on low incomes consider alternatives to equity release, for example by claiming benefits they may be entitled to but are not receiving. Equity release and trading down are two options of many, and older people may need advice as to whether they are the most effective option for them.

The financial advice market

Financial advice falls into two categories, generic advice and product-specific advice. Generic advice helps consumers to identify and understand their current financial position and needs, and helps them to plan their finances accordingly, but stops short of recommending a particular product. Because of this, it is unregulated, although the Financial Services Skills Council is in the process of developing industry performance standards for generic financial advice, as part of the FSA's work on financial capability (Financial Services Skills Council 2006).

In contrast, product-specific advice goes one step further, identifying a specific product for a client seeking financial advice, and is therefore regulated by the FSA. It can be delivered by independent or tied advisers:

1. *Independent* financial advisers (IFAs) offer a range of products from the whole market. They offer advice on a fee or commission basis.
2. *Tied* advisers offer advice on the products of one particular provider.
3. *Multi-tied* advisers offer advice on the products of a selection of providers, but not on the whole market.

Advice is currently inadequate for asset-rich, income-poor homeowners

Although it is particularly important that asset-rich, income-poor pensioners are able to seek financial advice, their options are very limited. Independent product-specific advice is expensive and of poor quality. And a market for generic financial advice does not yet exist. We explore these further below.

Why is the market failing to serve these pensioners? The underlying problem is that the cost of providing financial advice is related to adviser time rather than the value of the product bought.

Conversations with product providers and advisers suggest that it takes just as long, if not longer, to arrange an equity release product, as it does to arrange much larger loans in the form of conventional mortgages, or set up investment products and pensions. Thus, there are similar charges, even if the amounts of money involved in equity release loans are much smaller than for conventional mortgages and investments. As a percentage, these costs will be more significant than for other products. The market sets a high price for good quality financial advice because there are people, who are perhaps wealthier and buying a different kind of product, willing to pay it.

Others have argued that the people who are least well-served by markets in financial advice are those who do not earn enough to be profitable for the industry to advise, but who are, nevertheless, largely independent of welfare support and so do not receive financial counselling and advice from the state (The Resolution Foundation 2005). While this is true for *investment* decisions about how best to accumulate assets – those whose income is mostly comprised of welfare support are unlikely to benefit substantially from advice about how best to invest their income – it is not necessarily true for decisions about how to decumulate assets in older age.

Pensioners in receipt of benefits do not get financial advice from the state about the implications of releasing wealth from their home. Thus, the financial needs of low-income pensioners should be prioritised alongside the needs of younger individuals who are also unprofitable for the financial services industry.

Independent product-specific advice is expensive and poor quality

It was suggested in our seminars that the number of IFAs offering advice on equity release is insufficient to meet demand. In a survey of its members, which account for 95 per cent of the market share in equity release products, Safe Home Income Plans (SHIP) found that the majority felt that there was a shortage of specialist IFAs prepared to offer advice on equity release. Reasons identified included the amount of regulation, the fact that there is a longer sales process than for other products, the risks of mis-selling versus the rewards offered, and a lack of education and awareness about equity release (SHIP 2006b).

However, the availability of qualified (but not necessarily specialised) advisers does not appear to be a problem: there are enough advisers taking qualifications in equity release products, and enough firms who list equity release as one of their top areas of business.

In February 2006, 3,744 IFAs had taken the relevant qualifications in lifetime mortgages since their introduction in November 2004 (Chartered Institute of Insurance 2006, Institute of Financial Services 2006). The FSA has made these qualifications compulsory for all newly qualifying advisers offering advice on lifetime mortgages. Each qualified adviser would have only had to sell on average six to seven products in 2005 to meet the market volume of 26,654 (Key Retirement Solutions 2006), assuming all these products were sold through intermediaries (this represents an overestimate as many are actually sold directly from providers).

Looking at IFA firms, 1,746 of the 8,800 firms on the online listings site IFA Promotion had registered equity release as one of their top eight areas of business (IFA Promotion 2006). IFA Promotion contains 80 per cent of market share by number of firms (Kempson and Collard 2005). Market volume would only require each of these firms to have sold 15 to 16 products each year on average, again assuming all products were sold through intermediaries. Even though most IFA firms tend to be small (Mintel 2003), this is not a large number.

But when we phoned a selection of IFAs who had listed themselves on IFA Promotion as advising on equity release, many admitted that they actually had little experience of selling these products.

Evidence from the FSA suggests that the quality of financial advice in this area can be very poor. Because of its concerns in this area, the FSA conducted a 'mystery shopping' exercise of 42 IFAs, product providers and mortgage brokers in May 2005 (Financial Services Skills Council 2006). More than 70 per cent of financial advisers did not gather enough information about their customers before offering them advice on equity release, and 74 per cent failed to ask about benefit eligibility (see Box 8.1). It also found that lifetime mortgage consumers were being advised to borrow to invest the equity released in high-risk products unsuitable for their needs.

Box 8.1: The low quality of equity release advice currently available

The FSA's mystery shopping exercise, with 42 IFAs, product providers and mortgage brokers in May 2005 found:
- 70 per cent of advisers did not gather enough information about their customers before offering them advice on equity release.
- 79 per cent failed to ask whether customers had considered alternative methods of raising the required funds.
- 79 per cent failed to ask about health and life expectancy.
- 83 per cent failed to ask about preferences for the customer's estate.
- 83 per cent failed to ask whether customers had the need for a stable income.
- 64 per cent failed to ask about future life plans (for example, moving home).
- 74 per cent failed to ask about tax status.
- 83 per cent failed to ask about Pension Credit eligibility, and 74 per cent about eligibility for other benefits.
- 60 per cent failed to ask about other debt.
- 67 per cent failed to ask about savings and investment.
- Most advisers failed to discuss the terms and conditions of equity release schemes – 52 per cent did not explain what would happen if the customer or their partner died or went into a residential or care home, and 57 per cent did not explain what would happen if the customer wanted to move house later.

Yet 64 per cent said that the customer would be eligible or suitable for an equity release scheme.

Source: Financial Services Authority (2005c)

Many of the mystery shoppers involved in this exercise would have been mis-sold an equity release product.

These problems are not unique to the market for lifetime mortgages. Research for the Department for Work and Pensions (DWP) has shown that similar problems exist in the financial advice market for retirement planning (Kempson and Collard 2005). Although almost all of the 45 financial advisers interviewed in depth for this study said that they would offer advice to anyone who sought it, regardless of their income level, in practice, most of them advised very few people on low incomes, if at all.

Levels of knowledge about Pension Credit were low, although higher among tied and multi-tied agents than IFAs – many advisers had never even heard of Pension Credit. Very few said they felt able to advise clients on the implications of Pension Credit entitlement for retirement planning. Knowledge of Council Tax Benefit and Housing Benefit was even lower than that of Pension Credit.

Quality is not the only problem. Independent product-specific advice can also be very expensive, so consumers can end up paying significant fees for bad advice. It is difficult to produce a representative figure for the cost of financial advice, because costs can be opaque and there are different methods of paying for independent financial advice – on a fee basis, a commission basis, or a combination of the two.

According to IFA Promotion, typical hourly fees are in the region of £50 to £200. We phoned a random selection of 25 IFAs from five different areas listed on IFA Promotion. They quoted flat-rate fees that varied from £100 to £1,000, and hourly rates from £90 to £250. For an older person seeking to take out a small loan in the region of a few thousand pounds, an upfront fee in the region of a few hundred pounds is substantial.

There is little generic advice available

While independent product-specific financial advice is expensive and of variable quality, there is very little generic financial advice from trained specialists available to older people. There is ample generic *information* about releasing wealth from the home, available from different agencies such as Help the Aged, Age Concern and the FSA, detailed in Box 8.2. But generic information cannot fill the need for generic advice, personalised to each individual's situation. There is no generally available free source of personalised advice for older people seeking to release wealth from their homes.

Generic financial advice might not wholly be able to replace the need for consumers to seek the independent *product-specific* advice that the FSA recommends all consumers undertake before buying an equity release product. But it does have the potential to:

1. significantly reduce the potential for mis-selling of equity release products to some older people for whom they may not be appropriate

2. ensure that individuals are aware of the different kinds of product-specific advice available, and of the need to shop around for the best prices if buying from tied or multi-tied agents who do not source the whole market.
3. explore the appropriateness of equity release products or trading down for older people seeking to increase their income.

Nor is generic advice provided well by the market. The FSA Financial Capability Working Group on Generic Advice held a consultation on the provision of generic advice in 2004/05 (Financial Services Authority

---

Box 8.2: Information on releasing housing wealth is easy to find, but generic advice is not personalised

1. Factsheets
Age Concern, Help the Aged and the Financial Services Authority all publish free guides to equity release, available online and by post. These guides contain information about the different kinds of equity release available, alternative income-raising measures such as trading down, and the implications of equity release, including for benefit entitlement. Age Concern has also published a book on raising capital from the home. These organisations suggest that all those interested in taking out an equity release product seek financial advice.

2. Helplines
Age Concern and Help the Aged also operate free telephone helplines for older people. These helplines give out generic information from their factsheets, but do not offer advice tailored to an individual's situation.

3. Face-to-face information
Citizens Advice Bureaux (CAB) provide advice on a wide range of topics, including money advice and debt counselling. But they are not authorised to give clients financial advice under the Financial Services and Markets Act 2000 (Citizens Advice 2003, Paxton *et al* 2005), so cannot advise clients on the suitability of equity release products for their situations. In an FSA survey of CAB advisers, most said that if generic financial advice were to be offered in CAB, they would need extensive training (Financial Services Authority 2004). A small FSA and CAB pilot has provided *pro bono* advice from IFAs through the CAB network to clients (Widdowson 2005). Additionally, around 200 out of 400 of Age Concern's local branches provide general advice and information services, but like the telephone lines, this face-to-face service generally consists of replicating factsheet information – it does not constitute one-to-one generic advice (source: personal communication).

2005a). Respondents to the consultation gave a wide range of reasons as to why they thought the market had failed to fill the gap. On the demand side, they cited a lack of understanding of what financial advice had to offer and a resulting unwillingness to pay for advice, and a lack of trust of the financial services industry. On the supply side, reasons given included the difficulty of providing generic financial advice commercially to make a reasonable profit, or even break even, and a concern that generic financial advice could slip into regulated territory.

Improving the quality and availability of affordable financial advice

The lack of suitable advice should be an area of major concern for both government and industry. First, it means that equity release and trading down might be underexplored as options for pensioners who are asset-rich and income-poor, which has consequences for the Government's objective to reduce pensioner poverty. But, more significantly, it creates a real risk of mis-selling of equity release products.

Further impetus for government action is created because the complexity of the benefits system adds to the problem. Interaction with means-tested benefits makes it more difficult for older people to accurately assess whether releasing wealth from the home would be appropriate for them. Financial advice needs to cover the interface between financial products and the benefits system. But, as the FSA mystery shopping exercise and the DWP study of IFAs show, few financial advisers understand the basics of the benefits system, let alone its complexities.

Government needs to do two things. First, the FSA needs better regulation, so that, when people pay for financial advice, they should be able to reasonably expect a certain standard of service. Second, there is a role for government in expanding generic advice as a partial substitute for product-specific advice for those who cannot afford to pay for it.

Better regulation of product-specific advice

There is clearly a problem with current standards of paid-for advice services, as evidenced by the FSA's mystery shopping exercise. Despite the FSA regulation of IFAs that advise on lifetime mortgages, which has been in place since November 2004, standards appear to remain low.

There is scope for the FSA to improve its regulation of paid-for financial advice. Although the consumer benefits of regulation must be traded off against its costs, both to government and industry, the quality of product-specific advice means it is currently unfit for purpose and is in urgent need of improvement.

Current FSA regulation with respect to financial advice on lifetime mortgages is detailed in Section 8 of the FSA Handbook (Financial Services

Skills Council 2006). These regulations state that a financial adviser must take reasonable steps to ensure that a product is suitable for a client before selling it to them. This includes determining the impact on entitlement to benefits, on tax liabilities, and considering whether other options may be more appropriate, such as home reversion schemes or local authority grants.

This regulatory framework needs to be built upon further. The FSA should undertake an annual mystery shopping exercise, not simply to investigate the quality of financial advice on offer, but to act as a deterrent to advisers who may be cutting corners. The FSA has already taken a step towards this by clarifying that the evidence collected in mystery shopping research projects can be used for supervision and enforcement purposes in the Supervision Manual (Mystery Shopping Exercise) Instrument 2005 (Financial Services Authority 2005b). It is also in the process of undertaking a further mystery shopping exercise that will report in autumn 2006 (Financial Services Authority 2006).

The FSA needs to go further, however, by committing to undertake an annual exercise on a larger scale than that carried out in May 2005. Failure to adhere to FSA regulations in this exercise should result in penalties high enough to act as an incentive for IFAs to improve standards. The FSA should:

● undertake an annual mystery shopping exercise to incentivise underperforming advisers to improve standards.

A benefits calculator should be made available free online to all
Chapter 7 recommended that the complexity of the benefit system merits the creation of an online benefits calculator for pensioners as an interim measure before more fundamental reform. Such a calculator could also improve the quality of financial advice offered by intermediaries to those on benefits. Currently, benefits software for intermediaries exists, but it is expensive, as outlined above. For a single user, the first year annual licence and training fee is £611 including VAT, with each further user charged at £545.[10] Alternatively, financial advisers can purchase the software on a single-use, per-case basis, at a price of £53 including VAT. To a financial adviser charging in the region of £200-£300 for advice on equity release, covering this extra cost would add a significant amount onto the price.

A free online calculator could be used by financial intermediaries and a generic advice service, which we consider below, in addition to being used by pensioners themselves.

---

10. Pricing correct as of 11 April 2006, information from www.ferret.co.uk/data/downloads/get file.aspx?path=guides/notes/&item_id=gui-note-fintal3 and www.ferret.co.uk/fintal-aspx/index.aspx?menu=fintalppc

Increase the supply of generic advice as a partial substitute for product-specific advice

More regulation, while improving the standards of paid-for financial advice, cannot solve the problem that some people will not be able to afford to pay for financial advice, or may be unwilling to do so. There is a chance that more regulation might even push up the cost of regulated advice further.

An affordable or free generic advice service could fill this affordability gap. There is a strong case for government to step in. It is unprofitable for industry to supply such a service at a price that consumers are willing to pay. In the absence of commercial provision, there is little third-sector provision of personalised generic financial advice for similar reasons: cost, and fears of straying into regulated territory. The advice black hole increases the risk of a mis-selling scandal, and also means that equity release and trading down may be underexplored options for asset-rich, income-poor pensioners.

A national generic financial advice service could take advantage of economies of scale in training and instruments. For example, advisers could make use of software designed for older people looking to increase their income, which could automatically process information about benefit eligibility and tax liability. Although such a generic advice service could not recommend a particular product because of liability issues, it could help to establish whether equity release or trading down might be an appropriate financial decision for older people. It could give information about different product types, with typical market conditions, interest rates and charges to enable clients to shop around providers for the best deal.

Such a service would need to fit into two broader government agendas, on financial capability and 'third-age' information. The importance of improving financial capability for widening financial inclusion has been recognised by this Government, and the FSA's Working Group on Generic Advice has stated that it would like to see a network of generic financial advice services readily available throughout the UK, provided for free or at an affordable price (Financial Services Authority 2005a, HM Treasury 2004a). Consultations held by this working group have indicated that the lack of generic financial advice available for *all* client groups, not just older people, is of universal concern.

Several organisations have been calling for free or affordable generic advice to be available to lower-income consumers of all ages, including the National Consumer Council, Which and Citizens Advice (Citizens Advice 2006, Consumers' Association 2002, National Consumer Council 2003). This has culminated in an independent organisation, the Resolution Foundation, currently researching and costing a national generic advice service (The Resolution Foundation 2005). The needs of *older people* should feature prominently in the design of any such service.

A generic financial advice service would also need to be fully integrated into the third-age information agenda. Financial advice is only one element of a broader range of advice that older people may need to seek, and they should be directed to the appropriate advice service from a central service.

The Government has announced plans for such a third-age information service, 'Link-Age Plus', which would eventually deliver a 'Sure Start' one-stop approach to older people's services, including social services, the Pension Service, health services, housing and local voluntary sector organisations (Department for Work and Pensions 2005b, Social Exclusion Unit 2006). Financial advice needs to be built into this model. Financial advice should also be integrated with a broader advice service on housing options that Care and Repair advocate for older people (Mountain and Buri 2005).

What might such a generic financial advice service look like? It is beyond the scope of this project on housing wealth to develop a proposal for a generic financial advice service that serves all sectors of the population, especially as the Resolution Foundation is currently in the process of a much larger piece of work on generic financial advice. But there are a number of features that any financial advice aimed at *older people* should incorporate, which we explore below.

A generic financial advice service that can cater for older people

Which features would a generic financial advice service need to have so that it could cater for older people? There are three main issues that need highlighting with reference to this group: cost to the client, the delivery medium and the importance of branding.

Cost to the client

For older people, in particular, it is important that a generic financial advice service should be provided free at the point of delivery. There will always be asset-rich, income-poor pensioners who simply cannot afford to pay the upfront costs of financial advice, even if it is provided on a not-for-profit basis.

One way of circumventing this affordability problem might be to charge on a means-tested basis. We have rejected this option because it would add yet more complexity to an already very complex financial decision. Means-testing would probably cost more in administration than it would save for a service that is likely to cost well under £100 per user, and the relatively low uptake of means-tested pensioner benefits (Department for Work and Pensions and National Statistics 2006) suggests that it might put older people off using the service.

Delivery medium

Generic financial advice could be delivered in a number of ways – for example, face-to-face, over the telephone, via the internet, or through any combination of these methods. Which method is likely to be most suitable for older people, while still remaining cost-effective?

An advice service based primarily on the internet can be ruled out because older people tend to have limited internet access. In May 2005, only 20 per cent of those aged 65 or over had accessed the internet in the last three months (National Statistics 2005b). Additionally, there is some evidence that those who lack financial confidence and are on lower incomes prefer one-to-one advice: in a survey of low-income consumers, 50 per cent said they would prefer to receive one-to-one advice compared to other forms (Jones and Barnes 2002). Such advice would need to be delivered face to face or over the telephone.

Many commentators who responded to the FSA consultation on generic advice think that the best way to give advice is face to face (Financial Services Authority 2005a). This is supported by an evaluation of the Home Equity Conversion Mortgage scheme in the US (see Box 3.3), which found that most advisers providing advice for older homeowners on equity release were strongly opposed to telephone advice where it could be avoided, because of the difficulty of using printed materials and the inability to read homeowners' reactions to the information presented (Rodda *et al* 2000). But face-to-face advice may be difficult to attend for some people, especially those with limited mobility, those with caring responsibilities and those living in rural areas. Telephone advice would be more accessible.

A generic financial advice telephone line could build on the experience of other government advice services delivered over the telephone, such as NHS Direct, Consumer Direct and Community Legal Service Direct.

The evaluation of the Community Legal Service Direct pilot found that many people would not have sought help had the telephone advice service not been available (Hobson and Jones 2003). However, it also showed that telephone advice was unsuitable for certain groups who might have trouble understanding information on the telephone, including those with learning difficulties, language problems and mental health issues. This suggests that a combination of telephone and face-to-face advice may be necessary, especially as some older people may be vulnerable and prefer to receive advice in person.

Trust

A generic financial advice service would need to have strong independent branding if it were to cater for older people. Evidence from the focus groups conducted for this project suggested that older people would be sceptical of an advice service provided by government, and that they would find it much easier to trust a service with an independent brand, such as Citizens Advice. This is supported by evidence from a small FSA and Citizens Advice pilot in 2005 to provide *pro bono* advice from IFAs through the CAB network. It showed that service users rated the impartiality of the service highly (Widdowson 2005). An independently-branded service could also be linked to a trusted third-sector brand such as Citizens Advice, Help the Aged or Age Concern.

Funding

The costs of such a service would ultimately depend on demand, and on how much time it would take to advise an older person on appropriate ways of maximising their income. In pilots for the National Debtline, the cost per call was £62 including set-up costs, or £40 excluding these costs (Gardner and Wells 2003). This compares to a cost of £32 per call for ChildLine, a volunteer-operated service. Initial unpublished research carried out by McKinsey on behalf of the Resolution Foundation suggests that a national financial advice service offered through a combination of the internet, the telephone and face-to-face meetings would cost in the region of £29 per user, based on a service that has 750 telephone advisers and 1,050 face-to-face advisers.

Further research is needed to accurately establish the demand that such a service is likely to generate. Pensioners who are not living on low incomes are much less likely to use the service.

If we assume that around a quarter of the one million asset-rich, income-poor pensioners, who are living below the Age Concern Modest but Adequate income level, but who own more than £100,000 of equiv-alised housing wealth, use the service, this amounts to a yearly running cost of around £7.25 million. Care and Repair's 'Should I Stay Or Should I Go?' pilot suggested that each full-time adviser in a housing options advice serv-ice could help between 90 and 100 older people per year, which would require 2,500 telephone and face-to-face advisers, slightly more than the number allowed for in the Resolution Foundation estimates (Mountain and Buri 2005).

Could such a service be partly funded by voluntary contributions from industry? Precedent does exist. The National Debtline, a debt counselling telephone helpline, is run by the Money Advice Trust, a registered debt charity that is partly funded by the credit and finance industry. But a clear financial case for industry funding exists here, because the provision of debt consolidation advice helps the industry to recover outstanding debt (Gardner and Wells 2003).

While it is unlikely that a financial case exists to the same extent in the equity release industry, such a service would certainly be in the industry's interest. A financial advice service is unlikely to have a large direct impact on product sales, but sales could grow if it improves the very poor reputa-tion the industry suffers from (Gay 2004, Rowlingson and McKay 2005). Government should encourage industry to contribute voluntarily on this basis.

Another way in which the cost to government might be reduced is by encouraging IFA firms or individual IFAs to donate their time to the provi-sion of generic advice through a national advice service. The provision of *pro bono* advice has not developed organically in the financial services industry as it has in the legal profession (see Box 8.4). This is likely to be, in part, because the average IFA firm size is much smaller than in the legal profession, with 93 per cent of firms only employing one or two advisers (Mintel 2003).

However, an FSA and Citizens Advice pilot has shown that, on a small scale at least, *pro bono* work by IFAs can be an effective way of delivering generic financial advice (Widdowson 2005). This pilot ran in eight Citizens Advice Bureaux for eight months in 2005. In total, 244 enquiries were dealt with, 63 per cent of which were from those aged over 50. The service was primarily used by those on low and mid incomes, who would not have oth-erwise been able to access financial advice. Ninety-five per cent of users rated the service as 'very good' or 'good', and 79 per cent took action as a result of the advice they received.

Government could provide the infrastructure required to facilitate *pro bono* advice by making it possible for IFAs to donate time to a national generic advice service. In doing so, it would fulfil the function that LawWorks fills for the legal provision, effectively providing client-matching, training and insurance (see Box 8.4). It would build on the pilot outlined above, and fit with the Government's volunteering agenda (HM Treasury 2004c).

The success of this policy would be dependent on it generating sufficient interest from IFAs for it to be worthwhile. Initial evidence from the FSA/Citizens Advice pilot is promising. Feedback from participating IFAs was positive, and many said that it increased their awareness of problems faced by those who would not normally fall into their client group (Widdowson 2005). However, further work is needed to establish whether there would be enough IFA participation to establish a *pro bono* scheme on a wider scale.

Box 8.4: *Pro bono* work in the legal profession

Pro bono advice in the legal profession takes two forms:
● A donation of employee time by a legal firm.
● A donation of time by an individual solicitor or barrister.

Historically, many large law firms have provided *pro bono* advice, and some have specialised *pro bono* departments. There are three organisations that provide an infrastructure for smaller firms and individuals to undertake *pro bono* work: the Free Representation Unit (mainly student barristers), the Bar Pro Bono Unit (barristers) and LawWorks (solicitors) (Smith 2002).

LawWorks has around 2,000 lawyers carrying out *pro bono* work. It has a membership fee that ranges from £500 for an individual lawyer, to £5,000 for a large firm. In exchange, it provides the following benefits:
● Matching lawyers with referrals from advice organisations in the local area.
● Training on topics relevant for *pro bono* clients, such as debt counselling.
● Indemnity insurance.
● A Law Society waiver, needed for all lawyers who practise outside their normal workplace setting.

Conclusions

Pensioners need to seek independent financial advice before taking out equity release products, but good quality and affordable advice can be hard to find. There is a pressing need to fill this current gap, so as to avoid a potential mis-selling scandal and to ensure that equity release and trading down are not underexplored options for hard-up pensioners who own their homes.

More regulation of the paid-for financial advice sector would help to ensure that people paying for advice do receive advice of a minimum standard. As part of this, the FSA should commit to undertaking an annual equity release mystery shopping exercise on a wider scale than in May 2005. However, regulation alone cannot tackle the problem of affordability.

The time is right for government to fill the gap with a generic financial advice service – which might be called 'MoneyDoctor' – that can cater to the needs of asset-rich, income-poor pensioners. The Government should:

- establish 'MoneyDoctor', a generic financial advice service to cater for older people. This should be run through a combination of telephone and face-to-face advice, and carry strong independent branding.
- use this to facilitate independent financial advisers to work *pro bono*. In doing so, it would fulfil the function that LawWorks fills for the legal provision, effectively providing client-matching, training and insurance.
- encourage equity release providers and other financial services firms to support the scheme, as one way of reducing the widespread distrust of these products that is constraining take-up.

9. Trading down

Chapter 5 showed that trading down can be the most cost-effective and low-risk way of releasing housing wealth. Our qualitative research in Chapter 6 showed that it is also the most popular. This chapter looks at trading down in more detail, and finds:

- Half of low-income retired homeowners live in 'larger homes', meaning more than two rooms in addition to a kitchen, bathroom(s), one bedroom for the first one or two household members and one further bedroom for each further member.
- A substantial barrier to older retirees trading down is the lack of suitable housing to move into. As well as preventing older people from releasing housing wealth, this has wider social costs, preventing larger homes from being made available to the market.
- A second barrier is the logistical problem of moving.

In response, the Government should:

- Increase the supply of housing suitable for older people, by considering making housing for older people an explicit part of Section 106 agreements, making Lifetime Homes standards compulsory in new buildings, and bringing older people into the coalition for more house-building.
- Encourage asset-rich income-poor to trade down earlier, extend housing options advice and widen adaptation grants. This could be done as part of a financial health check at retirement.

However, the decision to move is difficult, and small changes at the margin are unlikely to have large effects.

Trading down to a smaller home is the traditional and, as our focus groups showed, most popular way to release housing wealth for retirement. This chapter looks at how many households could benefit from trading down, and examines the two main barriers that prevent them: lack of suitable local housing to move into, and, particularly for older people, logistical problems.

The decision to move to a smaller, cheaper, or retirement-suitable home is frequently a difficult one. As well as the financial costs, there are the social and psychological costs of relocation, and the emotional attachment to a family home is considerable. In the focus groups we held with asset-rich, income-poor retired people, most participants felt that financial incentives would not make a difference to their decision, although they would be taken up if offered. Other studies have also noted that the decision to move or stay put is a matter for serious consideration and deliberation (Mountain and Buri 2005), so may not be easily influenced.

The problem is not, then, a subset of the more general issue highlighted by Barker of 'over-consumption of housing due to its role purely as an asset' (Barker 2004: 17). Older people are unlikely to be staying in their homes primarily to accumulate equity gains. The more important barriers in this context are those that prevent people from moving who would otherwise like to. Policies that *enable* people to trade down, rather than persuade them to, are likely to be more effective, and are the focus for this chapter.

For that reason, we do not look in detail at stamp duty as a disincentive to move – although we have noted elsewhere that, in the long run, moving to a tax on value instead of transactions appears to offer many advantages (Maxwell and Vigor 2005). If charged on the underlying value of land, rather than any construction on top of it, a reformed tax could also improve incentives for planners (McLean 2005) and increase macroeconomic stability (Muellbauer 2005).

Half of low-income retired homeowners live in larger homes

Our analysis of the English Longitudinal Study of Ageing suggests that 'under-occupancy' is fairly widespread among lower-income pensioners (Sodha 2005). The term should be treated with caution, as the data say nothing about the specific needs of individuals or the size of the rooms. But it is possible to get an idea of the potential size of the group who could benefit from easier trading down.

We define 'under-occupancy' in two ways, as having more than either two or three rooms in addition to a kitchen, bathroom(s), and one bedroom for the first one or two household members and one further bedroom for each further member. More than three extra rooms can therefore be thought of as more than two reception rooms and one spare bedroom, or more than one reception room and two spare bedrooms.

As shown in Figure 9.1, about half of older people living in poverty have more than two extra rooms, and a quarter have more than three extra rooms. The 21st percentile income level is approximately equivalent to 60 per cent of national median income, the most commonly used poverty threshold (see Sodha 2005).

Approaching the question from the other direction, those who move into privately owned sheltered accommodation do appear to free up larger homes. Sheltered housing builders McCarthy and Stone conducted telephone interviews in July 2003 with 512 prospective buyers who had expressed interest in retirement housing, but were still living in

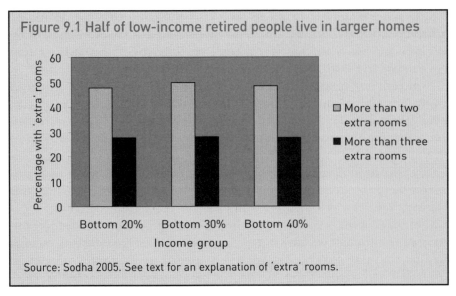

Figure 9.1 Half of low-income retired people live in larger homes

Percentage with 'extra' rooms

- □ More than two extra rooms
- ■ More than three extra rooms

Income group — Bottom 20%, Bottom 30%, Bottom 40%

Source: Sodha 2005. See text for an explanation of 'extra' rooms.

conventional accommodation. They found that 56 per cent were currently living in family-sized properties, 30 per cent were living in bungalows, and 12 per cent were living in flats. Seventy-one per cent agreed 'I do not need to live in a house as big as the one I currently live in'.

Similarly, a survey of 1,000 current residents of sheltered accommodation found that 45 per cent sold their properties to families or young couples (McLaren and Hakim 2003).

Although homeowners should derive some benefit from trading down, because they will have a smaller property that should be cheaper to manage, much of the benefit will depend on how much wealth they are able to release. It is important to be realistic about how much scope there is for trading down, and that the potential for increasing the number of people doing so may be limited.

The Pensions Commission estimated that trading down from a semi-detached house to a terraced one would release almost £25,000 in England and Wales, equivalent to around 30 per cent of the implicit value of the state pension. This figure falls to £20,000 in Greater London, although it exceeds £45,000 in the North West (Pensions Commission 2004). However, unpublished research by Steve Wilcox found that there is often little difference in average price between two- and three-bedroom houses for homes at the bottom end of the market. In 2004, the difference was less than £10,000 in 80 out of 416 local authorities in Great Britain for two- and three-bed houses at the lowest property value quartile. For lowest decile prices, the difference was less than £10,000 in 131 out of 416 local authorities.

In addition, these figures do not include the transaction costs of moving, including estate agents, conveyance fees and (for homes above the tax-free threshold) stamp duty.

The potential for retired homeowners in less expensive homes to release equity by moving to smaller properties in the same area therefore appears to be quite limited. As our focus groups showed, older homeowners may be reluctant to move to a cheaper property in a less expensive area, because they are often understandably keen to live near people they know, and in an area with which they are familiar. They are also keen to maintain at least one spare room.

Older people are often unable to find appropriate housing to move into

Housing suitable for retirement is not a fixed category. For some, 'suitable' may mean in accordance with the 'Lifetime Homes' standards developed by the Joseph Rowntree Foundation (Carroll *et al* 1999). These give 16 accessibility requirements, including, for example, minimum door widths, guideline heights for switches and sockets, and space for a stair lift. Individual requirements at any one time will vary, but those moving house at a time of declining mobility benefit from having a house that can at least be adapted for reduced mobility in the future. For others, 'suitable' may mean sheltered housing – generally small, self-contained units, with a resident warden. 'Extra care' sheltered housing generally offers meals, help with domestic tasks and some personal care.

The overlap of moving for mobility requirements with moving to release housing wealth is only partial, as moving into a more suitable home for retirement may require moving into a property of equal or even greater value.

Undersupply affects retirement-suitable housing

The surveys from McCarthy and Stone (McLaren and Hakim 2003) suggest their own clients found there was insufficient supply of private sheltered housing:

- 39 per cent of private sheltered housing residents had had to look 'further afield than I would have liked to find suitable accommodation as there was not enough in my area' (44 per cent disagreed).
- 66 per cent agreed 'when moving it is important for me to stay within my local area' (31 per cent disagreed).
- 81 per cent agreed 'there should be more of this type of accommodation available in my area' (12 per cent disagreed).

Similarly, the evaluation of the housing options service 'Should I Stay Or Should I Go?' noted that some participants who had made the decision to move found themselves with nowhere suitable to move to. Frustration with waiting for appropriate housing to become available was also expressed by housing options workers (Mountain and Buri 2005).

Databases of retirement-suitable housing confirm that the problem is a lack of availability, rather than older people's inability to find it. An online database provided by the Elderly Accommodation Council includes 'descriptions of almost all housing developments in the UK that cater specifically for older people' (Housing Care 2006). On 31 January 2006, this had 1,628 properties for sale, and 320 to rent.

Similarly, www.mobilityfriendlyhomes.co.uk is a dedicated online marketplace for properties that are accessible and/or suitably adapted to meet the needs of people with disabilities. On 31 January 2006, this had a total of 62 properties nationwide, with 25 in the South East, six in the South, and only a single property in London. The list of dedicated agents included eight in the South East, one in the West Midlands – and none in any other region.

So, it appears that there is a genuine shortage of suitable housing, rather than older people being unable to find suitable housing on the market. McCarthy and Stone (McLaren and Hakim 2003) concluded that, by 2020, there is likely to be a shortage of around 62,500 private sheltered housing units, based on the expected growth in the number of older people and constant levels of building.

The national underavailability of sheltered housing is made worse by its uneven distribution. The Social Exclusion Unit (2006) reported that coverage of extra-care housing for over 65 year olds ranged from no units per 1,000 people in one area to 30 per 1,000 in another. The report also noted that older people in rural areas have spoken about the difficultly of finding suitable sheltered accommodation in the areas in which they have lived for many years.

For trading down to be a viable option for all older people, there must be a reasonable choice of housing available to move into in every area. Older people, even more than other groups, depend on networks of family and neighbours for informal care (Bowling *et al* 2003, Coulthard *et al* 2002), and so are more constrained than most in their choice of location. This was a recurring theme in our qualitative research, in which all respondents were reluctant to move to a new area, and stressed the value they placed on living close to family and friends.

Additionally, consultations carried out by the Social Exclusion Unit (2006) led it to conclude that, at present, there is a shortage of specialist housing outside the social rented sector. This is a problem that will get worse as the number of home-owning older people increases.

If the low supply of retirement-suitable housing were simply due to low demand given the price, then the market would be working and there would be no need for concern. But that is not the case. Undersupply in the market for housing for older people is a result of the unusual nature of housing as a consumer good, government failures introduced through the planning process, and the general unresponsiveness of the UK housing market to prices.

The most salient difference between housing and most other consumer goods is that houses are durable – they provide a stream of 'housing services' without being used up, and can be resold to provide housing to others (for a wider review of the differences between houses and other goods, see HM Treasury (2005a)). The number of new houses built each year is equivalent to around one per cent of the total stock, so new build homes make up only a small proportion of supply: sales of new homes account for around ten per cent of all housing market transactions (Barker 2003). As a result, the available supply is slow to adapt to changing demands such as the need for retirement-suitable housing.

The unfettered operation of supply and demand is further disrupted by market interventions created by the planning process, which restricts the supply of land, the time taken to build housing, and types of housing that may be built. Refusals for planning permissions for major housing developments, for instance, have gone up from 15 per cent in 1996-99 to 25 per cent in 2002 (Tunnell *et al* 2004). These may well be socially useful interventions overall, but they mean that the relative lack of retirement-suitable housing is not necessarily a result of unwillingness to pay on the part of potential consumers.

Partly as a result of the factors outlined above, the supply of housing in the UK is relatively unresponsive to prices. It is only half as responsive as the French housing market, a third as responsive as in the US, and only a quarter as responsive as in Germany (Swank *et al* 2002, quoted in Barker 2003). Historically, the UK housing market has become *less* responsive over time: it was up to four times as responsive before World War II as it was throughout most of the post-war period, and it fell to almost zero in the 1990s (Malpezzi and Maclennan 2001, Meen 2003, quoted in Barker 2003).

The undersupply of retirement housing also has social costs

Amid concerns about the low and unresponsive level of housing supply (Barker 2003, 2004), it is often suggested that much of the existing stock could be better used – and that older single people, in particular, often continue to live in family-sized homes that are no longer appropriate to their needs (Holmes 2003). Because 99 per cent of the effective housing supply consists of resale stock (Muellbauer 2005), even a small improvement in how this is used can have a large effect relative to changes in the supply of new build homes. Making it easier for those older people who would like to move to a smaller home to do so would therefore have an impact on overall supply.

Similarly, a more efficient allocation of housing could reduce the negative environmental consequences of house building. The construction industry produced 10 million tonnes of waste in the UK in 2003, equivalent to one third of the waste produced by households (National Statistics 2005a). The construction and demolition industries together were responsible for creating 21 per cent of the hazardous waste in the UK, and, including the production and transport of construction products and materials, are responsible for about 10 per cent of national energy consumption (Environment Agency 2005).

Less quantifiable externalities include the shared interest in green land, pleasant views, and other intangible environmental goods represented in the planning regulations.

Better policy could make more suitable homes available

2005-06 has seen welcome policy advances

The planning process has recently been the focus of government attention. For example, Planning Delivery Grants, which aim to speed up planning decisions, were allocated £170 million in 2005-06, £135 million in 2006-07 and £120 million in 2007-08 (HM Treasury and ODPM 2005).

There has also been a focus on planning for older people's housing more specifically. The Treasury-commissioned inquiry into housing supply, conducted by Kate Barker (2004), suggested a review of the Planning Policy Guidance that relates to housing, and a draft 'Planning Policy Statement 3' was opened for consultation from December 2005 to February 2006.

The new statement will require sub-regional housing market assessments that identify the particular accommodation needs and demands of older people. Criticisms have been made that the importance of older people was underplayed: they were mentioned only once in the report, alongside other groups such as gypsies and travellers, key workers, homeless households, as well as black and minority ethnic groups and disabled people (Care and Repair England 2006).

Further changes to planning were made in January 2006. The Social Exclusion Unit (SEU) report *A Sure Start to Later Life: Ending Inequalities for Older People* announced the following actions:

14) The Office of the Deputy Prime Minister (ODPM), working with the Department of Health (DH), Department for Environment, Food and Rural Affairs (DEFRA) and external partners, will develop a strategy for housing and older people by 2006/7.

15) The Office of the Deputy Prime Minister (ODPM) will ensure that the housing needs of older people are built into the Housing

Diversity Action Plan to be published in late 2006.

16) As part of the Disabled Facilities Grant review and work on individual budgets, Ministers from the Office of the Deputy Prime Minister (ODPM), Department for Environment, Food and Rural Affairs (DEFRA) and Department of Health (DH) will lead a working group to consider how a more integrated delivery system for aids, adaptations and assistive technology policy can be developed.

17) The Office of the Deputy Prime Minister (ODPM) will build the lifetime homes standard into the Code for Sustainable Homes to ensure quick progress on increasing take-up of the lifetime homes standard.

Social Exclusion Unit 2006: 13-14

These are welcome developments, but there is room for more action. Possible ways forward are outlined below.

Incorporate Lifetime Homes in new build standards

Opportunity Age, a review of services for older people, announced 'a view to legislating by 2007 to incorporate the Lifetime Home Standards' as mandatory for all new homes (Department for Work and Pensions 2005b: 35).

Yet, a consultation on the Code for Sustainable Homes proposed placing Lifetime Homes standards in the discretionary category, which 'homes built to higher Code standards *may* have' (ODPM 2005b: 8). The forthcoming strategy for housing and older people, promised in the SEU report quoted above, should, therefore, take a much stronger line on Lifetime Homes, making them compulsory for new buildings.

Planning regulations

Discussion with house builders suggested that the planning process is geared heavily towards affordable housing, at the expense of housing for older people. Both should be a concern of government – particularly as increasing the availability of housing for older people could free up family homes, with consequences for the rest of the housing market.

Section 106 agreements could include more provision for retirement-appropriate houses

'Section 106' agreements allow local authorities to secure contributions from developers to mitigate the impact of development under the terms of the Town and Country Planning Act 1990. Section 106 has been widely used to provide social housing in order to preserve mixed communities.

Section 106 could also be used to provide retirement-suitable housing. Insofar as mixed communities are an important objective, new developments will need to be accompanied by more provision for older people if the community balance is to be maintained – in exactly the same way that new developments need to be accompanied by more affordable housing provision for those on low incomes.

Any reforms to Section 106 would take place alongside other planned changes necessitated by the introduction of planning-gain supplement. A consultation was launched at the Pre-Budget Report (HM Treasury 2005b) that suggested refocusing Section 106 agreements according to a 'development-site environment' approach. This is expected to involve ruling out contributions to, for example, education, health, leisure or cultural facilities, but leaving in contributions for a 'mix of housing types' and design coding. Explicitly included is the provision of affordable housing. A call to widen the types of properties included should not be seen as an endorsement of Section 106 as a long-term mechanism for encouraging local amenities and socially desirable housing development.

Further steps could include:

- Allowing Section 106 agreements to contribute to the construction costs of dedicated retirement housing, such as sheltered housing and extra-care housing, on a nearby (but different) site. This is in danger of being disallowed under the proposed 'development-site environment' approach.
- Counting owner-occupied retirement-suitable housing towards targets on affordable housing.

The introduction of a trade-off between affordable (working-age) housing and housing for older people may prove problematic. It would appear as if less housing was available for the working-age population. Yet this would be an illusion: as argued above, building more retirement-suitable housing allows older people to trade down, thereby freeing up larger homes.

Logistical help is needed for older pensioners

Logistical problems are more acute for older people

Older pensioners (those 75 and above) may have additional difficulties finding a house, dealing with logistical necessities such as surveys and legal fees, and arranging the physical move itself. Commercial services may be unavailable or mistrusted, meaning that individually and socially efficient trades fail to take place.

The difficulties of moving house are particularly pronounced for widows in the current generation of older pensioners, many of whom have had little experience of financial management. A survey by the Financial Services Authority (2002) found that women had a different attitude to finances generally, and to long-term finances in particular. For some, there was a tendency to rely on the husband for these matters, and this was particularly true for older women (those close to or above retirement age). In some instances, women were simply unaware of financial plans and were not involved in decision-making.

Advising older people on the logistical process of moving was mentioned in Chapter 6. One of the key challenges is ensuring that decisions about housing are taken sufficiently early.

Adaptation grants should be extended

Lifetime Homes Standards are an important first step, but they are a long-term solution. New buildings make up a small proportion of total supply, so the availability of retirement-suitable housing can only be significantly improved by adapting the stock of existing houses.

As in other areas, there have been recent policy advances developments, but there is room for more action. As part of the Government's drive to help people stay in their own home, the Supporting People programme has co-ordinated several funding streams into a single budget, and has made grants independent of tenure. The programme was launched in April 2003 to bring together all services for those who need support to live more independently. In the three years since, it has invested £5 billion, with 1.2 million users (ODPM 2005d).

Part of the Supporting People programme involves channelling more money to Home Improvement Agencies (HIAs), also referred to as 'Care and Repair' agencies or 'Staying Put' schemes. These are usually managed by housing associations, local authorities, charities, or an independent management committee, and aim to 'enable those in need of support to maintain their independence in their chosen home for the foreseeable future' (Foundations 2006).

Also available under current policy is a Disabled Facilities Grant, currently being reviewed by the Department of Health, the Department for Education and Skills, and the Office of the Deputy Prime Minister (Social Exclusion Unit 2006).

The grant is available for essential adaptations to give disabled people better freedom of movement into and around their homes and to access essential facilities within it. This can mean, for example, widening doors and installing ramps, installing a stair lift or a downstairs bathroom. The local authority must be convinced that the adaptations are 'necessary and appropriate' for the individual, as well as 'reasonable and practicable' depending on the age and condition of the property. Grants are means tested, and are limited to £25,000 in England and £30,000 in Wales (ODPM 2005c).

This is a good base to work from. Further improvements could be made in three areas. First, the coverage of HIAs and similar services in England is incomplete. There are HIAs in 300 local authorities in England (Foundations 2006), leaving 88 authorities without coverage. In contrast, all 22 Welsh local authorities have an agency (Care and Repair Cymru 2006), and in Scotland all local authorities have a Care and Repair scheme in operation apart from Mid Lothian (Care and Repair Scotland 2006). The scale of these agencies is typically very small, often three to four staff covering a large area.

Second, HIAs could broaden their mission, from adapting current properties to finding and adapting new ones. An individual whose current home is assessed as unsuitable could then choose help in the form that suits them best:

- Adapting their current property.
- Adapting a different property to move into.
- Moving into a property that is already suitable.

An option that includes moving would offer the homeowner the possibility of releasing some equity, and possibly freeing up a larger home for others. Strict assessment of need might rule them ineligible, but the resulting social benefit of freeing up a larger home might outweigh the cost of the subsidy. This would also fit with the current trend towards individualised budgets (for adults, Department of Health 2005, and for children's services, HM Treasury and Department for Education and Skills 2005).

The legal framework for extending local authority assistance has already been created by the Regulatory Reform (Housing Assistance) (England and Wales) Order 2002. This allows local authorities to provide assistance to any person for the purpose of 'enabling him to acquire living accommodation', where they are satisfied that 'that the acquisition of other living accommodation would provide for that person a benefit similar to that which would be provided by the carrying out of work of any description in relation to his existing living accommodation' (Article 3).

However, a recent evaluation of the impact of the Regulatory Reform Order (RRO) found that the capacity of local government to deliver its provisions is severely limited, with many authorities not employing enough staff to enable them to meet their responsibilities under the RRO and the Housing Act 2004 (Groves and Sankey 2005).

The challenge, then, is ensuring that local authorities have the capacity to make use of this provision where appropriate, and that central government tools, such as the Disabled Facilities Grant, also allow a more flexible approach.

Third, budgets must be protected. The budget for Supporting People was cut by 1.7 per cent in nominal terms in the 2005 Pre-Budget Report, the fourth year in a row that the budget for these services was reduced.

Conclusions

As noted in Chapter 6, older people are more receptive to releasing housing wealth through trading down than through equity release. Approximately half of older households in poverty have larger homes, meaning more than two spare rooms in addition to a kitchen, bathroom(s), and one bedroom for the first one or two household members and one further bedroom for each further member. Around a quarter of older people in poverty have spare capacity if the definition is more than three extra rooms.

Trading down is easier earlier, when the logistical problems are less acute. Therefore the Government should:

- encourage 'financial health checks' at retirement that include looking at housing options, and make clear where appropriate the benefits of moving early.

Trading down, particularly by the 'old old', is restricted by an inadequate supply of housing to move into, and by logistical problems. Given the large stock of housing relative to new supply, there are no quick fixes. But to help overcome the problem of availability, the Government should:

- highlight the importance of an adequate housing supply for older people in the new version of the Planning Policy Statement 3.
- make housing for older people an explicit part of Section 106 agreements, as part of the reform process accompanying the introduction of planning-gain supplement.
- make Lifetime Homes standards compulsory in new buildings.
- bring older people into the coalition for more house building. Taking retirement housing into account, we can no longer draw a simple picture of established owners preventing development that would ruin their view, at the expense of would-be first-time buyers. Instead, the undersupply of housing creates losers among established groups too.

To help overcome logistical problems for the 'old old', the Government should:

- provide logistical help with the process of trading down, building on the lessons learnt in Should I Stay or Should I Go? pilots and elsewhere (Mountain and Buri 2005).
- widen adaptation grants, by extending the remit of home improvement agencies to include housing options and move on services.

- find ways to ensure that Supporting People funding is fairly allocated to services that meet the needs of retired low-income homeowners.

10. Conclusions and policy recommendations

Housing wealth is important, and it will become more so. Historically, it has been an excellent investment for those who have been able to own, and, by 2003, accounted for just over 50 per cent of net personal wealth (HM Revenue and Customs 2006b).

But the role that housing wealth can play has been overstated. With respect to improving access to housing wealth, the priority should be an assets ladder, rather than a housing ladder. If the motivation is fairness and equality, the first task should be to help those at the very bottom. The community benefits of housing wealth also appear weaker than the community benefits of a wider spread of basic financial capital. And homeownership for those on lower (and more variable) incomes is riskier and less profitable than for the rest of the population.

Later in life, the potential of housing wealth to meet other needs is relatively restricted. A house provides rent-free living in retirement, but, for the vast majority of homeowners, a house should not be thought of as a pension.

That said, for those who do want to release wealth from their home in retirement, there are important barriers that government can help to overcome. Means testing in the benefits system unfairly penalises the transfer of wealth from housing to liquid savings, and should be reduced. Financial advice available to older people wanting to buy equity release products is expensive and often of low quality. As such, there is a strong argument for government provision of generic financial advice for older people in order to fill this gap. Older people's ability to trade down is limited because there are not enough suitable properties available to trade down into. Moreover, the logistical process of moving, particularly for the 'old old', can trap asset-rich, income-poor pensioners in unsuitable homes.

For first timers, prioritise an assets ladder, not a housing ladder

Government support for homeownership is often justified in terms of people's aspirations to own their home, but aspirations alone do not provide a sufficient case for intervention. This report has focused on arguments specific to the nature and effects of housing wealth, rather than all aspects of housing policy. In particular, it looked at the effectiveness of homeownership policies as a way of tackling wealth inequality, whether homeownership leads to different patterns of thought or behaviour, and whether these in turn make mixed-tenure communities a desirable end in themselves.

Housing wealth has been a self-reinforcing driver of wealth inequality. This makes the distribution of housing wealth an important concern for society. To a more limited extent, the state has an interest in the distribution of housing wealth because it can provide resources in retirement. But, beyond rent-free living, housing wealth does little to support living standards, as the cost of converting wealth to income is extremely high.

However, the unequal distribution of housing wealth is not necessarily best tackled directly through subsidising people to get on the housing ladder. The key drivers that have made homeownership profitable have been increases in land value, and the nature of mortgage-financed homeownership, which pre-commits people to save and delivers large gains when house prices rise faster than interest rates. These second two drivers both bring extra risks that may not be suitable for people on lower incomes. Returns on homeownership are typically lower for low-income households.

Furthermore, the psychological and community benefits of homeownership have often been overstated. Many of these benefits, such as increased security and propensity to plan, appear to flow more from smaller-scale financial assets than from housing wealth. Homeownership does appear to increase the amount of control one has over one's environment, although it is hard to trace this through to other kinds of community benefits.

Some have also suggested that community-level benefits include increased political participation, higher educational attainment and better neighbourhood upkeep. But the evidence is not robust, and the causal mechanisms and outcomes themselves are open to question. This does not undermine the case for 'mixed communities' in a wider sense, but suggests that a narrow focus on the community benefits of homeownership is misguided.

We should therefore think in terms of an assets ladder, rather than a housing ladder, and the underlying concerns may be better addressed through financial wealth. The Government should:

- ensure that those on low incomes have decent incentives to save, perhaps through a national rollout of the Saving Gateway pilots.
- place debate on housing within the wider context of the transmission of wealth inequality across generations.

In terms of policy for encouraging mixed income communities, this means creating opportunities for different income groups to buy in the same area – but not necessarily subsidising them. The Government should:

- continue to ensure that new developments have a mix of tenure.
- exercise caution in how mixed communities are achieved on existing estates. Artificially shifting tenants into homeownership cannot be expected to deliver the benefits of mixed communities: mixed tenure is a consequence, not a cause, of mixed communities.

Don't let the ladder become a 'down' escalator

Although fair access to financial wealth should be the first priority, housing policy must not allow homeownership to be pulled further out of reach of those at the margin. If this is not addressed, the bottom rungs of the asset ladder will become a down escalator, forcing those at the bottom to move faster simply to stay in the same position relative to homeowners.

Widening access to homeownership cannot just be about giving subsidies to those who could not otherwise afford it. As long as house prices continue their dizzying rate of growth, homeowners will continue to gain at the expense of non-owners. Plausible levels of house building in the South East are unlikely to meet demand, so regional policy must take a new priority. The Government should:

- use the charged issue of homeownership to increase the priority the public gives to regional policy.

Other research by ippr has shown that there is more that the Government can do to address the regional imbalance by making housing supply and demand a more explicit element of decisions that affect the regions, including on infrastructure and policies to encourage entrepreneurship (Adams *et al* 2003, Adams and Reed 2006 forthcoming).

Reducing the rate of house price growth is an ambitious goal. But, well in advance of achieving it, we must recognise its implication: housing can become more affordable, or it can stay profitable, but it cannot be both. Once house price growth falls below the rate of mortgage interest, every pound of mortgaged housing equity costs money. Large mortgages may still be desirable, as they allow the homeowner to live in a more expensive home, but, if house price growth falls below mortgage rates, then mortgages will not pay for themselves through capital appreciation. If the Government expects to meet its affordability targets, it should:

- refrain from encouraging those on lower incomes to take out large mortgages, or to think of homeownership as primarily an asset-building strategy.

Ensure a fair distribution for those left behind

In the past, housing has been very profitable largely because of the unearned increment in housing wealth gains. It is the value of land, not buildings, that has made housing more expensive over time, and this has not been as a result of any action by landowners. Estate agents implicitly recognise this point when they say the key factors are 'location, location, location' – but the determinants of value are social, depending on local amenities rather than the landowner. The private appropriation of publicly-created wealth should not go unchallenged.

As a medium-term alternative to a fair tax on windfall land value, the Government should:

- use the introduction of planning-gain supplement to establish the principle that land value is socially created.
- ensure that the windfall nature of house price rises is fully understood ahead of any losses (or market corrections).
- respond to criticisms of stamp duty and inheritance tax by making it clear that recent house price gains have created losers as well as winners, and that taxation of windfall housing wealth is a fair way of paying for the measures needed to address this gap.

For old timers, reduce the barriers to releasing housing wealth, but recognise that a house is not a pension

One fifth of the retired living in poverty own more than £100,000 of housing wealth. This amounts to 440,000 retired people, 4.4 per cent of the overall retired population, each owning an average of £177,000 of housing wealth, or £77.1 billion in total. Housing wealth is likely to become even more important for today's middle-aged generation as they reach retirement, if, as predicted, levels of pensioner homeownership increase and more couples remain childless. But there is a danger that housing wealth is overcommitted: not all the housing wealth owned by asset-rich, income-poor pensioners can be released, and it cannot fill the funding gaps of pensions, care needs, property upkeep, and housing supply.

Households need to recognise that their house is not their pension. The process of releasing wealth from the home is expensive, so only a small proportion can be accessed; trading down will provide only limited funds unless the move is from mansion to bedsit; and our research with the current generation of pensioners suggests that they have deep-seated objections to equity release.

To help those pensioners who do want to release wealth from their home, the Government has a duty to help remove the barriers that it has inadvertently erected, particularly in the complex system of means-tested benefits for older people. The Government could also help by improving the availability of financial advice, ensuring that there is an adequate supply of suitable housing for retirees, and helping older pensioners with the logistical process of moving.

Reduce means testing and complexity

For many pensioners on means-tested benefits, converting wealth from one type (housing) to another type (savings) results in a reduction in their benefits. Our calculations show that almost a million pensioners, 8.2 per cent, own more than £100,000 of equivalised housing wealth, but are on means-tested benefits. Because of the extreme complexity of the benefits system, a much larger group are unaware of exactly how their benefits would be affected, and are unable to calculate whether they would be penalised.

As debate unfolds following the report of the Pensions Commission and the 2006 Pensions White Paper, these problems again highlight the importance of simplicity in benefits and pensions. They further strengthen the already substantial case for eliminating means-tested Pension Credit, as recommended in previous ippr work (Brooks *et al* 2002, Paxton *et al* 2005). The Government should:

- eliminate Pension Credit and replace it with a non-means-tested British State Pension at the level of guarantee credit (£114.05 per week for a single pensioner in 2006-07).

In the interim, the Government should:

- make available a free, online benefits calculator for pensioners so they can calculate the effects of increasing their income or capital on their benefit eligibility. This should be simple and transparent, so it can be used by individuals and financial intermediaries alike.

Increase the availability of advice

The complexity of the benefits system makes it particularly important that there is good quality, affordable financial advice for older people interested in releasing wealth from their home. This can help reduce the risk of mis-selling of equity release products to a potentially vulnerable group. It can also help to ensure that those who would benefit from it are able to take it up with confidence. Yet there is inadequate financial advice available for asset-rich, income-poor pensioners. Independent, product-specific advice is expensive and of such variable quality that it cannot be relied upon. Free, generic financial advice is not widely available.

Government has two tasks. First, product-specific advice must be improved. The Government should:

- undertake an annual mystery shopping exercise, through the FSA. This would act as a deterrent to advisers who may be cutting corners, and provide regular snapshots of advice quality.

Second, there must be more generic financial advice for asset-rich, income-poor pensioners. Generic financial advice is personal to the individual, but stops short of recommending specific products and brands. Current resources available to older people consist almost exclusively of information, such as that provided by Age Concern, Help the Aged and the FSA. While useful, this is not tailored to the individual. This situation can be remedied. The Government should:

- establish 'MoneyDoctor', a generic financial advice service, to cater for older people. This should provide a combination of telephone and face-to-face advice, and carry strong independent branding.
- use this service to facilitate *pro bono* work by independent financial advisers, by providing client matching, training and insurance. In doing so, it would fulfil the function that organisations such as LawWorks fulfil for the legal provision.
- encourage equity release providers and other financial services firms to financially support the service, as one way of reducing the widespread distrust of these products, which is constraining take-up.

Increase the availability of housing suitable for retirement

Trading down is the most cost-effective and low-risk way of releasing wealth from the home. Our qualitative research showed that it is also the most popular. Half of low-income retired homeowners live in 'larger homes', meaning at least three rooms, in addition to a kitchen, bathroom(s), one bedroom for the first one or two household members and one further bedroom for each further member.

Yet, a lack of suitable housing to move into is a substantial barrier to older pensioners who would like to trade down. As well as preventing older people from releasing housing wealth, this has wider social costs, stopping larger homes being made available to the market.

The Government should:

- highlight the importance of an adequate housing supply for older people in the new version of the Planning Policy Statement 3.
- make housing for older people an explicit part of Section 106 agreements, as part of the reform process accompanying the introduction of planning-gain supplement.
- make Lifetime Homes standards compulsory in new buildings.

Help with the logistical process of moving

Trading down is also restricted because older people, especially older pensioners, often have problems with the logistical process of moving. One answer is to ensure that pensioner households consider their housing needs at an early stage, and that it is made clear to asset-rich, income-poor retirees that they would benefit from trading down earlier. The Government should:

- encourage financial health checks at retirement that include looking at housing options, and making clear, where appropriate, the benefits of moving early.

Those who are already older, and need help moving house, could benefit from more government action. As well as increasing the incomes of poor pensioners, this would free up larger homes. The Government should:

- provide logistical help for the process of trading down, building on the lessons learnt in the 'Should I Stay or Should I Go?' pilots and elsewhere
- widen adaptation grants, by extending the remit of home improvement agencies to include housing options and move-on services.
- ensure that Supporting People funding is fairly allocated to services that meet the needs of retired low-income homeowners.

Aside from these four sets of actions – on benefits, advice, housing supply, and the practical side of trading down – there is not a strong case for government actively supporting the market for equity release. The cost of equity release is high, but interest rates now overlap with standard mortgages, and the risks for the providers are greater and cash flow lower than in standard mortgages. The current generation of pensioners is highly distrustful, but this is better addressed by improving financial advice than by attempting to influence their decision-making. Direct support for equity release would also further distort individual long-term saving decisions, diverting saving from pensions into houses.

Housing is an asset like no other. It has fed wealth inequality, transmitting disadvantage from one generation to the next. At the same time, those who do want to use housing wealth in older age face high costs to doing so. This book argues that the answer does not lie in subsidies at either end of the lifecycle, either supporting first-time buyers or subsidising the release of equity. Instead, the Government should be prioritising an assets ladder over a housing ladder, to ensure that the necessary steps before homeownership are easier for those on low incomes; and it should facilitate the release of wealth by reducing the tangled complexity of the benefits system. Housing wealth can provide many benefits, and be spent on many things, but it cannot do everything. For too long, its potential has been overstated.

References

Aaronson, D (2000) 'A note on the benefits of homeownership', *Journal of Urban Economics*, 47 (3) 356-69.

Ackerman, B and Alstott, A (1999) *The Stakeholder Society* New Haven: Yale University Press

Adams, J and Reed, H (2006 forthcoming) *A Northern Economic Agenda* London: Institute for Public Policy Research

Adams, J, Robinson, P, and Vigor, A (2003) *A New Regional Policy for the UK* London: Institute for Public Policy Research

Age Concern (2002) *Modest But Adequate – A Reasonable Living Standard for People Aged 65-74: Age Concern's Summary and Policy Conclusions* London: Age Concern

Age Concern (2003) *Equity Release and Income-Related Benefits from October 2003 Onwards*. Age Concern Fact Sheet IS/7 London: Age Concern England

Alliance and Leicester (2005) *Attitudes of First Time Buyers in the 21st Century* Leicester: Alliance and Leicester Group Ltd.

Atkinson, R and Kintrea, K (2001) 'Disentangling area effects: evidence from deprived and non-deprived neighbourhoods', *Urban Studies*, 38 (12) 2277-98.

Bandura, A (ed.) (1995) *Self-efficacy in Changing Societies* Cambridge: Cambridge University Press

Banks, J, Emmerson, C, Oldfield, Z and Tetlow, G (2005) *Prepared for Retirement? The Adequacy and Distribution of Retirement Resources in England* London: Institute for Fiscal Studies

Barker, K (2003) *Barker Review of Housing Supply: Securing Our Future Housing Needs. Interim Report* London: HM Treasury and Office of the Deputy Prime Minister

Barker, K (2004) *Barker Review of Housing Supply: Securing Our Future Housing Needs. Final Report* London: HM Treasury and Office of the Deputy Prime Minister

Berube, A (2006) 'Overcoming barriers to mobility: the role of place in the United States and the UK', in Delorenzi, S (ed.) *Going Places: Neighbourhood, ethnicity and social mobility* London: Institute for Public Policy Research

Blum, T and Kingston, P (1984) 'Homeownership and social attachment', *Sociological Perspectives* 27 (2) 159-80

Böheim, R and Taylor, M (1999) *Residential Mobility, Housing Tenure and the*

Labour Market in Britain Colchester: Institute for Labour Research, University of Essex

Bowling, A, Sutton, SR , and Bannister, D (2003) *Adding quality to quantity: Older people's views on quality of life and its enhancement* London: Economic and Social Research Council

Bramley, G, Morgan, J, Cousins, L, Dunmore, K with MORI Social Research (2002) *Evaluation of the Low Cost Home Ownership Programme* London: Office of the Deputy Prime Minister

Bramley, G and Karley, NK (2005) *Homeownership, Poverty and Educational Achievement* Edinburgh: Heriot Watt University

Brewer, M and Emmerson, C (2003) *Two Cheers for the Pension Credit?* IFS Briefing Note 39, London: Institute for Fiscal Studies

Briault, C (2006) 'Delivering Change: Our Plans for Financial Capability.' Speech at FSA Establishing a Baseline and Delivering Change Seminar, London: Financial Services Authority

Brooks, R (2005) 'Commentary', in Maxwell D and Vigor A (eds.) *Time for Land Value Tax?* London: Institute for Public Policy Research 54-60

Brooks, R, Regan, S and Robinson, P (2002) *A New Contract for Retirement* London: Institute for Public Policy Research

Brown, G (2005) Speech by the Rt Hon Gordon Brown MP, Chancellor of the Exchequer at the launch of the Government's consultation document on housing, 'Homebuy: Expanding the opportunity to own'

Brown, G (2006) 'Chancellor of the Exchequer's Budget Statement', London: HM Treasury

Burholt, V and Windle, G (2006) *The Material Resources and Well-Being of Older People* London: Joseph Rowntree Foundation

Burrows, R (2003) *Poverty and Home Ownership in Contemporary Britain* Bristol: Policy Press

Burrows, R and Wilcox, S (2004) *Low-income homeowners in Wales* York: Joseph Rowntree Foundation

Bynner, JM and Paxton, W (2001) *The Asset-Effect* London: Institute for Public Policy Research

Cappellari, L and Jenkins, SP (2003) 'Transitions between unemployment and low pay', *Quaderni Dell'istituto Di Economia Dell'impresa E Del Lavoro* Universit' Cattolica Del Sacro Cuore (36)

Care and Repair Cymru (2006) www.careandrepair.org.uk/aboutus/ History1374.html (accessed 05.02.06)

Care and Repair England (2006) *Consultation Paper on a New Planning Policy Statement 3 (PPS3) Housing,* Nottingham: Care and Repair England

Care and Repair Scotland (2006) www.care-repair-scot.org.uk/index.html (accessed 07.03.06)

Carroll, C, Cowans, J, and Darton, D (eds.) (1999) *Meeting Part M and Designing Lifetime Homes* London: Joseph Rowntree Foundation

Chartered Institute of Insurance (2006) Personal communication to the authors

Citizens Advice (2003) *Citizens Advice Information System* London: Citizens Advice

Citizens Advice (2006) *Treasury Select Committtee Enquiry into Financial Inclusion* London: Citizens Advice

Clark, T (2002) *Rewarding Saving and Alleviating Poverty? The Final Pension Credit Proposals*. IFS Briefing Note No 22, London: Institute for Fiscal Studies

Commission on Sustainable Development in the South East (2005) *Commission on Sustainable Development in the South East Final Report* London: Institute for Public Policy Research

Conservative Party (2006) *Built to Last* London: Conservative Party

Consumers' Association (2002) *National Financial Advice Network: Policy Paper* London: Consumers' Association

Coulthard, M, Walker, A , and Morgan, A (2002) *People's Perceptions of Their Neighbourhood and Community Involvement: Results from the Social Capital Module of the General Household Survey 2000* London: The Stationery Office

Council of Mortgage Lenders (2005) *Equity Release and the Impact on Benefits and Tax* London: Council of Mortgage Lenders

Council of Mortgage Lenders (2006) 'Table IR2A: Mortgage and related interest rates', London: Council of Mortgage Lenders

Council of Mortgage Lenders and Ferret (2004) *FINTAL: Lifetime Mortgages and Benefits Calculation and Advice System* London: Council of Mortgage Lenders

Cox, K (1982) 'Housing tenure and neighbourhood activism', *Urban Affairs Quarterly*, 18 (1) 102-29

Curry, C (2004) *Pensions or Property?* London: Pensions Policy Institute

Department for Work and Pensions (2003) *Households Below Average Income 1995/95–2002/03* London: The Stationery Office

Department for Work and Pensions (2004a) *Households Below Average Income 2003/04* London: The Stationery Office

Department for Work and Pensions (2004b) *Client Group Analysis of the Population over State Pension Age November 2004* London: The Stationery Office

Department for Work and Pensions (2005a) *Households Below Average Income 2003/04* London: Department of Work and Pensions

Department for Work and Pensions (2005b) *Opportunity Age: Meeting the Challenges of Ageing in the 21st Century* London: The Stationery Office

Department for Work and Pensions and National Statistics (2006) *Income Related Benefits Estimates of Take-Up in 2003/2004* London: National Statistics

Department of Health (2005) *Independence, Well-being and Choice: Our Vision for Adult Social Care in England* London: The Stationery Office

Di, ZX (2003) *Housing Wealth and Household Net Wealth in the United States: A New Profile Based on the Recently Released 2001 SCF Data* (Joint Center for Housing Studies Working Paper WO03-8) Cambridge: Harvard University

Di, ZX, Yang, Y, and Liu, X (2003) *The Importance of Housing To the Accumulation of Household Net Wealth* (Joint Center for Housing Studies Working Paper W03-5) Cambridge: Harvard University

DiPasquale, D and Glaeser, EL (1999) 'Incentives and social capital: are homeowners better citizens?' *Journal of Urban Economics* 45 (2) 354-84

Doling, J and Stafford, B (1989) *Home Ownership: The diversity of experience* Aldershot: Gower

Dowding, K, De Wispelaere, J, and White, S (2003) *The Ethics of Stakeholding* Basingstoke: Palgrave Macmillan

Edwards, L (2005) *Home Truths: The Reality Behind Our Housing Aspirations* London: Shelter

Edwards, L, Regan, S, and Brooks, R (2003) *Age Old Attitudes? Planning for Retirement, Means-Testing, Inheritance and Informal Care* London: Institute for Public Policy Research

Environment Agency (2005) *Sustainable Construction: Position Statement* Bristol: Environment Agency

Equity Release Working Party (2005) *Equity Release Report 2005* London: The Actuarial Profession

Farlow, A (2004) 'UK house prices: a critical assessment', paper given at Credit Suisse First Boston Housing Market Conference, London, 12 May 2003

Financial Services Authority (2002) 'The Impact of an Ageing Population on the FSA', *FSA Consumer Research 10* London: Financial Services Authority

Financial Services Authority (2004) *Widening the Scope? FSA and CAB Research into Delivering Financial Advice Through the CAB* London: Financial Services Authority

Financial Services Authority (2005a) *Financial Capability: Developing the Role of Generic Financial Advice* London: Financial Services Authority

Financial Services Authority (2005b) *Handbook Notice 49* London: Financial Services Authority

Financial Services Authority (2005c) *Equity Release – Mystery Shopping Results* London: Financial Services Authority

Financial Services Authority (2006) *Major Thematic Work H1 2006* London: Financial Services Authority

Financial Services Skills Council (2006) *The Development of National Occupational Standards for Providers of Generic Financial Advice* London: Financial Services Skill Council

Ford, J and Quilgars, D (2001) 'Failing home owners? The effectiveness of public and private safety nets', *Housing Studies*, 16 (2) 147-62

Foundations (2006) www.foundations.uk.com (accessed 05.02.06)

Frederick, S, O'Donoghue, T, and Loewenstein, G (2002) 'Time discounting and time preference: a critical review', *Journal of Economic Literature* 40 (2) 351-401

Galster, G (1983) 'Empirical evidence on cross-tenure differences and community satisfaction', *Journal of Social Issues*, 28 (3) 107-19

Galster, G (1987) *Homeownership and Neighborhood Reinvestment* Durham, NC: Duke University Press

Gardner, C and Wells, J (2003) *Evaluation of the Money Advice Debtline Pilot and Business Case for Development of 'National Debtline'* London: Deloitte & Touche

Gay, M (2004) *Retirement Realities: Shocked and Struggling* London: National Consumer Council

Gibbons, S, Green, A, Gregg, P and Machin, S (2005) 'Is Britain pulling apart? Area disparities in employment, education and crime', in Pearce, N and Paxton, W (eds.) *Social Justice: Building a Fairer Britain* London: Politico's/ Institute for Public Policy Research

Gibbons, S and Machin, S (2005) 'Paying for Primary Schools: Supply Constraints, Popularity or Congestion', paper given at Royal Economic Society's Annual Conference, University of Nottingham, 22 March 2005

Green, G, Grimsley, M, and Stafford, B (2005) *The Dynamics of Neighbourhood Sustainability* York: Joseph Rowntree Foundation

Green, RK and Hendershott, PH (2001) 'Home-ownership and unemployment in the US', *Urban Studies* 38 (9) 1509-20

Green, RK and White, MJ (1997) 'Measuring the benefits of homeowning: effects on children', *Journal of Urban Economics* 41, 441-61

Groves, R and Sankey, S (2005) *Implementing New Powers for Housing Sector Renewal* London: Joseph Rowntree Foundation

Hansard (2004) HC vol 422, col 1258W London: The Stationery Office

HBOS Plc (2006) 'Historical data spreadsheet', www.hbosplc.com/economy/ historicaldataspreadsheet.asp (accessed 12.4.06)

Heseltine, M (1979) 'House of Commons Debates 15.5.79 Col. 80', London: The Stationery Office

Hills, J, Smithies, R, and McKnight, A (2006) *Tracking Income: How Working Families' Incomes Vary Through the Year* London: London School of Economics

HM Revenue and Customs (2006a) 'Table 13.5: Distribution Among the Adult Population of Marketable Wealth (series C)', available at www.hmrc.gov.uk/stats/personal_wealth/table13_5.pdf

HM Revenue and Customs (2006b) 'Table 13.1 Identified Personal of Wealth of Individuals in The United Kingdom, Year of Death Basis' available at www.hmrc.gov.uk/stats/personal_wealth/13_1_delay_mar06.pdf

HM Treasury (2004a) *Promoting Financial Inclusion* London: The Stationery Office

HM Treasury (2004b) 'Home Reversion Plans To Be Regulated', Press Notice 45/04, London: HM Treasury

HM Treasury (2004c) *Budget 2004: Prudence for a purpose* London: The Stationery Office

HM Treasury (2005a) *The Government's Response to Kate Barker's Review of Housing Supply* Norwich: The Stationery Office

HM Treasury (2005b) *Planning-Gain Supplement: a Consultation* London: The Stationery Office

HM Treasury and Office of the Deputy Prime Minister (2005) *Housing Policy: an Overview* London: HM Treasury

HM Treasury and Department for Education and Skills (2005) *Support For Parents: The Best Start for Children* London: The Stationery Office

Hobson, J and Jones, P (2003) *Methods of Delivery Telephone Advice Pilot Evaluation Report* London: Community Legal Service

Holmes, C (2003) *Housing Equity and Choice* London: Institute for Public Policy Research

Housing Care (2006) www.housingcare.org/jargonbuster.aspx (accessed 31.01.06)

IFA Promotion (2006) Personal communication to the authors

Institute of Financial Services (2006) Personal communication to the authors

Johnstone, S (2005) *Private Funding Mechanisms for Long-Term Care* London: Joseph Rowntree Foundation

Joint Centre for Scottish Housing Research (2005) *CORE: Annual Digest 2004/05* St Andrews: The Housing Corporation

Jones, P and Barnes, T (2002) *Would You Credit It? People Telling Stories About Credit* London: Citizens' Advice

Jones, R (2004) 'The true cost of moving', *The Guardian*, 17 January 2004, 'Money' section

Kelly, G and Lissauer, R (2000) *Ownership for All* London: Institute for Public Policy Research

Kempson, E and Collard, S (2005) *Advice on Pensions and Saving for Retirement: Qualitative Research with Financial Intermediaries*. Department for Work and Pensions Research Report No 289 Leeds: Corporate Document Services

Kempson, E, McKay, S, and Collard, S (2005) *Incentives to save: Encouraging Saving Among Low-Income Households*. Final Report on the Saving Gateway Pilot Project Bristol: Personal Finance Research Centre, University of Bristol

Key Retirement Solutions (2006) *UK Equity Release Monitor Q4 2005: More than £1bn Worth of Equity Release Plans Sold for Second Consecutive Year* Preston: KRS

Labour Party (2005) *Britain Forward not Back* London: Labour Party

Lakoff, G (2004) *Don't Think of an Elephant: know your values and frame the debate – the essential guide for progressives* Vermont: Chelsea Green Publishing

Low Cost Home Ownership Taskforce (2003) *A Home of My Own: The Report of the Government's Low Cost Home Ownership Task Force* London: Housing Corporation

Lyons Inquiry into Local Government (2005) *Consultation Paper and Interim Report* London: HM Treasury

Malpezzi, S and Maclennan, D (2001) 'The long-run price elasticity of supply of new residential construction in the United States and the United Kingdom', Journal of Housing Economics, 10 (3) 278-306.

Maxwell, D and Vigor, A (eds) (2005) *Time for Land Value Tax?* London: Institute for Public Policy Research

Mayer, N (1981) 'Rehabilitation decisions in rental housing', *Journal of Urban Economics*, 10, 76-94

McLaren, J and Hakim, M (2003) *Report: A Housing Needs Strategy Specific to Meeting the Needs of the Elderly* Bournemouth: McCarthy and Stone Plc.

McLean, I (2005) 'Politics of the land tax – then and now', in Maxwell D and Vigor A (eds.) *Time for Land Value Tax?* London: Institute for Public Policy Research

Meade, J (1964) *Efficiency, Equality and the Ownership of Property* London: George Allen and Unwin

Meen, G (2003) 'Regional Housing Supply Elasticities in England: work commissioned by the Barker Review', unpublished

Meyer, P, Yeager, J, and Burayidi, M (1994) 'Institutional myopia and policy distortions: the promotion of homeownership for the poor', *Journal of Economic Issues*, 28 (2) 567-76

Mintel (2003) *Advice and Independent Intermediaries, Post-Depolarisation* London: Mintel

Mountain, G and Buri, H (2005) *Report of the Evaluation of Pilot Local Housing Options Advice Services for Older People* Sheffield: Sheffield Hallam University

Muellbauer, J (2005) 'Property taxation and the economy', in Maxwell D and Vigor A (eds.) *Time for Land Value Tax?* London: Institute for Public Policy Research

National Consumer Council (2003) *Simplified Investment Products: A response to the Financial Services Authority and Treasury consultations* London: National Consumer Council

National Statistics (2005a) 'Total waste arisings by industrial sector and type of waste expressed in million of tonnes', available at www.statistics.gov.uk/ STATBASE/ssdataset.asp?vlnk=5329 (accessed 13.4.06)

National Statistics (2005b) *Adults Who Have Used the Internet in Three Months Prior to Interview by Sex/Age (Great Britain),* available at www.statistics.gov.uk/StatBase (accessed 13.4.06)

National Statistics (2005c), *Benefit Payments and Uprating of RPI: Uprating of Benefits Payments,* available at www.statistics.gov.uk/CCI/nugget.asp?ID=204 &Pos=1&ColRank=1&Rank=160 (accessed 5.9.05)

Nicholas, A, Povey, D, Walker, A and Kershaw, C (2005) *Home Office Statistical Bulletin: Crime in England and Wales 2004/2005* London: Home Office

O'Regan, KM and Quigley, JM (1996) 'Spatial effects upon employment outcomes: the case of New Jersey teenagers', *New England Economic Review,* May/June, 41-58

Office of the Deputy Prime Minister (2005a) *HomeBuy – Expanding the Opportunity to Buy* London: The Stationery Office

Office of the Deputy Prime Minister (2005b) *Proposals for introducing a Code for Sustainable Homes: A Consultation Paper* London: Office of the Deputy Prime Minister

Office of the Deputy Prime Minister (2005c) *Disabled Facilities Grants* London: Office of the Deputy Prime Minister

Office of the Deputy Prime Minister (2005d) *Creating Sustainable Communities: Supporting Independence. Consultation on a Strategy for the Supporting People Programme* London: Office of the Deputy Prime Minister

Office of the Deputy Prime Minister (2005e) *HomeBuy: Expanding the Opportunity to Own, Final Regulatory Impact Assessment (RIA) September 2005* London: Office of the Deputy Prime Minister

Office of the Deputy Prime Minister (2005f) *Autumn Performance Report 2005* London: Office of the Deputy Prime Minister

Office of the Deputy Prime Minister (2005g) *HomeBuy: Expanding the Opportunity to Own, Consultation Paper, April 2005, Supporting Document* London: Office of the Deputy Prime Minister

Office of the Deputy Prime Minister (2005h) *Sustainable Communities: Homes for All. A Five Year Plan from the Office of the Deputy Prime Minister* London: The Stationery Office

Office of the Deputy Prime Minister (2005i) *Housing in England 2003/04, Part 1: Trends in Tenure and Cross-Tenure Topics* London: The Stationery Office

Oswald, AJ (1996) 'A Conjecture on the Explanation for High Unemployment in the Industrialized Nations: Part I' *University of Warwick Working Paper No. 475*, Warwick: University of Warwick

Oswald, AJ (1997) 'Thoughts on NAIRU', Correspondence to *Journal of Economic Perspectives*, 11, 227-28

Paxton, W (2002) *Wealth Distribution – the Evidence* London: Institute for Public Policy Research

Paxton, W (ed.) (2003) *Equal shares? Building a progressive and coherent asset-based welfare policy* London: Institute for Public Policy Research

Paxton, W, Pearce, N, and Reed, H (2005) 'Foundations for a progressive century', in Pearce, N and Paxton, W (eds.) *Social Justice: Building a Fairer Britain* London: Politico's/Institute for Public Policy Research

Paxton, W, White, S, with Maxwell, D (2006) *The Citizen's Stake* Bristol: Policy Press

Pensions Commission (2004) *Pensions: Challenges and Choices – The First Report of the Pension Commission* London: The Stationery Office

Pensions Commission (2005) *A New Pension Settlement for the Twenty First Century, Second Report of the Pensions Commission* London: The Stationery Office

Perkins, D, Florin, P, Rich, R, Wandersman, A and Chavis, D (1990) 'Participation and the social and physical environment of residential blocks: crime and community context', *American Journal of Community Psychology*, 18, 83-115

Preston, G (2005) *Helter Skelter: Families, disabled children and the benefit system* (CASE Paper 92) London: CASE

Regan, S and Paxton, W (2003) *Beyond Bank Accounts* London: Institute for Public Policy Research

Rodda, D T, Herbert, C, and Lam, H-K (2000) *Evaluation Report of FHA's Home Equity Conversion Mortgage Insurance Demonstration: Final Report* Washington: US Department of Housing and Urban Development

Rohe, WM and Stewart, LS (1996) 'Homeownership and neighbourhood stability', *Housing Policy Debate* 7(1) 37-81

Rohe, WM, McCarthy, G, and Van Zandt, S (2000) *The social benefits and costs of homeownership: A critical assessment of the research* Washington DC: Research Institute for Housing America

Rossi, P and Weber, E (1996) 'The social benefits of homeownership: empirical information from national surveys', *Housing Policy Debate*, 7 (1) 1-36

Rowlingson, K and McKay, S (2005) *Attitudes to Inheritance in Britain* York: Joseph Rowntree Foundation

Safe Home Income Plans (SHIP) (2006a) 'SHIP Full Year Results 2006', SHIP Press Release, 30 January, Preston: SHIP

Safe Home Income Plans (SHIP) (2006b) 'Education and Awareness Amongst Advisers Critical Say Equity Release Providers', SHIP Press Release, 28 January, Preston: SHIP

Safe Home Income Plans (SHIP) (2006c) 'SHIP Member Survey: Equity Release Industry Predicts Consumers will be the Big Winners in 2006', SHIP Press Release, 21 January, Preston: SHIP

Saunders, P (1979) *Urban Politics* London: Hutchinson

Saunders, P (1990) *A Nation of Homeowners* London: Unwin Hyman

Sherraden, M (1991) *Assets and the Poor: A new American welfare policy* New York: ME Sharpe, Inc

Smith, J (2004a) 'Understanding demand for home ownership: aspirations, risks and rewards', in Council of Mortgage Lenders (ed.) *Housing Finance* London: Council of Mortgage Lenders

Smith, J (2004b) *CML Housing Finance Autumn 2004: Exploring Attitudes to Housing Wealth and Retirement* London: Council of Mortgage Lenders

Smith, R (2002) 'Pro Bono Legal Services in England and Wales ', paper given at Odgoode Hall Legal Aid Roundtable, Toronto, 1 November

Social Exclusion Unit (2006) *A Sure Start to Later Life: Ending Inequalities for Older People* London: The Stationery Office

Sodha, S (2005) *Housing-Rich, Income-Poor: The Potential of Housing Wealth in Old Age* London: Institute for Public Policy Research

Speak, S and Graham, S (1999) 'Service not included: private service restructuring, neighbourhoods and social marginalisation' *Environment and Planning A*, 31 (11) 1985-2001

Sproule, J, Roy, A, and Rose, J (2004) *ABI Life Insurance Monthly November 2004* London: The Association of British Insurers

Stewart, MB (1999) *Low pay, no pay dynamics. Persistent Poverty and Lifetime Inequality: The Evidence*, Proceedings of a workshop at HM Treasury, 17-18 November 1998 (published in Hills, J (ed) *CASEreport 5*) London: London School of Economics and HM Treasury

Sunstein, CR and Thaler, RH (2003) *Libertarian Paternalism is Not an Oxymoron* Washington DC: Brookings Institute

Swank, J, Kanes, J, and Tieman, A (2002) 'The housing ladder, taxation, and borrowing constraints', *De Nederlandsche Bank Staff Reports*, 1-26

Tatch, J (2006) 'Will the real first time buyers please stand up?' *Housing Finance*, Q3, 1-16

The Resolution Foundation (2005) *Decisions: The Social Value of Financial Advice* London: The Resolution Foundation

Thomas, B and Dorling, D (2004) *Know your place: housing wealth and inequality in Great Britain 1980-2003 and beyond* London: Shelter

Tribal HCH (2005) *Homebuy financial modelling – initial outputs. Version 2* London: Tribal HCH

Tunnell, C, White, N, and Hyams, K (2004) *Investigating the Increasing Volume of Planning Appeals in England* London: Office of the Deputy Prime Minister

Van Parijs, P (1995) *Real Freedom for All: What (If Anything) Can Justify Capitalism?* Oxford: Oxford University Press

Wanless, D (2006) *Securing Good Care for Older People: Taking a Long Term View* (The Report of the Wanless Social Care Review) London: The King's Fund

Widdowson, B (2005) *Financial Advice Pilot Project Evaluation Report* London: Citizens' Advice

Wilcox, S (2005) *UK Housing Review 2005-6*, 14

Wilson, JQ and Kelling, GE (1982) 'Broken windows: the police and neighborhood safety', *Atlantic Monthly*, March

Yadama, G and Sherraden, M (1996) 'Effects of assets on attitudes and behaviours: advance test of a social policy proposal', *Social Work Research*, 20 (1) 1-64